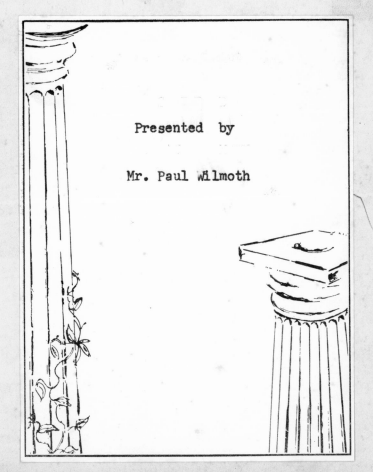

Presented by

Mr. Paul Wilmoth

Fiorello!

A new musical

Book by

Jerome Weidman

and

George Abbott

Music by

Jerry Bock

Lyrics by

Sheldon Harnick

Random House
New York

Photographs by courtesy of Eileen Darby-Graphic House

FIORELLO! *was first presented by Robert E. Griffith and Harold S. Prince at The Broadhurst Theatre, New York City, on November 23, 1959, with the following cast:*

(in order of appearance)

ANNOUNCER	Del Horstmann
FIORELLO	Tom Bosley
NEIL	Bob Holiday
MORRIS	Nathaniel Frey
MRS. POMERANTZ	Helen Verbit
MR. LOPEZ	H. F. Green
MR. ZAPPATELLA	David Collyer
DORA	Pat Stanley
MARIE	Patricia Wilson
BEN	Howard Da Silva
FIRST HACK	Stanley Simmonds
SECOND HACK	Del Horstmann
THIRD HACK	Michael Quinn
FOURTH HACK	Ron Husmann
FIFTH HACK	David London
SIXTH HACK	Julian Patrick
SEEDY MAN	Joseph Toner
NINA	Pat Turner
FLOYD	Mark Dawson
SOPHIE	Lynn Ross
FIRST HECKLER	Bob Bernard
SECOND HECKLER	Michael Scrittorale
THIRD HECKLER	Jim Maher
FOURTH HECKLER	Joseph Toner
THEA	Ellen Hanley
SENATOR	Frederic Downs
JUDGE CARTER	Joseph Toner
COMMISSIONER	Michael Quinn

POLITICIAN	H. F. Green
MITZI	Eileen Rodgers
FRANKIE SCARPINI	Michael Scrittorale
FLORENCE	Deedy Irwin
REPORTER	Julian Patrick
FIRST MAN	Scott Hunter
SECOND MAN	Michael Scrittorale
TOUGH MAN	David London
DERBY	Bob Bernard
FRANTIC	Stanley Simmonds

SINGERS: David Collyer, Barbara Gilbert, Del Horstmann, Deedy Irwin, Mara Landi, David London, Julian Patrick, Ginny Perlowin, Patsy Peterson, Silver Saundors, Ron Husmann.

DANCERS: Charlene Carter, Bob Bernard, Elaine Cancilla, Ellen Harris, Patricia Harty, Scott Hunter, Bob La Crosse, Lynda Lynch, James Maher, Gregg Owen, Lowell Purvis, Dellas Rennie, Lynn Ross, Dan Siretta, Michael Scrittorale, Pat Turner.

Production directed by George Abbott
Choreography by Peter Gennaro

Scenery, costumes and lighting by William *and* Jean Eckart
Musical direction: Hal Hastings
Orchestrations by Irwin Kostal
Dance music arranged by Jack Elliott

SYNOPSIS OF SCENES

ACT ONE
New York City, shortly before World War I.

ACT TWO
Ten Years later.

MUSICAL NUMBERS

ACT ONE

"On the Side of the Angels"
> BOB HOLIDAY, NATHANIEL FREY, PATRICIA WILSON

"Politics and Poker" HOWARD DA SILVA and POLITICIANS

"Unfair" TOM BOSLEY, PAT STANLEY and GIRLS

"Marie's Law" PATRICIA WILSON and NATHANIEL FREY

"The Name's LaGuardia" TOM BOSLEY and COMPANY

"The Bum Won" HOWARD DA SILVA and POLITICIANS

"I Love a Cop" PAT STANLEY

"I Love a Cop" reprise PAT STANLEY and MARK DAWSON

"Till Tomorrow" ELLEN HANLEY and COMPANY

"Home Again" COMPANY

ACT TWO

"When Did I Fall in Love" ELLEN HANLEY

"Gentleman Jimmy" EILEEN RODGERS and DANCING GIRLS

"Gentleman Jimmy" reprise COMPANY

"Little Tin Box" HOWARD DA SILVA and POLITICIANS

"The Very Next Man" PATRICIA WILSON

"The Very Next Man" reprise PATRICIA WILSON

Finale

PROLOGUE

After the "Overture" the orchestra plays a few bars of the "Marine Hymn."

ANNOUNCER Ladies and gentlemen, His Honor Fiorello H. La Guardia, Mayor of New York.

FIORELLO *(Voice)* Well, children, I guess you've been wondering what's happened to little Shirley Shorthand. Patience and fortitude!
(The lights come up gradually. FIORELLO *is sitting in a radio station, holding up a comic paper. Above his head an electric sign reads* "ON THE AIR." *He is talking into a microphone marked* "WNYC")

FIORELLO In this first box we see Shirley leaving for the office. Her mother stands in the door. Mrs. Shorthand says: "Goodbye, Shirley dear, be a good girl." Now in this next box what do we see? Oh, ho! A fierce-looking fellow—Shirley's boss—Alderman P. T. Pickel, a very, very corrupt man. And I can remember when we had a lot of corrupt men running our dear city—way back before the First World War, when I had my law office in Greenwich Village...
(The lights begin to fade. The stage is in total darkness as we hear NEIL's *voice)*

ACT ONE

Scene One

Time: Shortly before the First World War.

Place: Law offices of FIORELLO H. LAGUARDIA *in Greenwich Village. Two simple rooms: a private office at left; a combination reception room and outer office at right.*

At rise: It is late afternoon. NEIL, *the bright young law clerk, is at the switchboard.* MORRIS, *the doleful, resigned, pessimistic office manager, is standing near the filing cabinets, talking on the phone.* MRS. POMERANTZ, *a plump, squat matron in her fifties, is seated on the client's bench.*

NEIL *(Into switchboard phone)* Yes, I'll give him the message. *(Switchboard buzzes)* Office of Fiorello H. LaGuardia, good afternoon. *(He listens, then turns)* Morris, on Saperstein versus Kriewald, General Sessions, Tuesday—will Mr. LaGuardia be there?

MORRIS I don't think so.

NEIL You're kidding.

MORRIS Mr. LaGuardia never has time for people who pay their bills. He'll be taking care of some charity case.

NEIL Aw—come on.

MORRIS   Sure, he'll be there.
   (MR. LOPEZ, *a shabbily dressed man, enters and looks around*)

MR. LOPEZ   Excuse—?

MRS. POMERANTZ   I'm waiting first!

NEIL (*Into phone*)   Yes, sir. Yes, he'll be there.
   (*He hangs up and makes a note on his pad*)

MR. LOPEZ   My papers. I got trouble.
   (*Buzzer sounds.* MR. ZAPPATELLA, *an elderly Italian, enters*)

NEIL (*To* LOPEZ)   One second, please. (*Into phone*) Office of Fiorello H. LaGuardia.

MRS. POMERANTZ (*To* ZAPPATELLA)   I'm waiting first.

NEIL (*To* ZAPPATELLA)   Just have a seat, please. (*To* MORRIS) Morris, it's your wife.

ZAPPATELLA   Excuse—

MORRIS (*Picking up phone*)   Yes, Shirley?

ZAPPATELLA (*To* NEIL)   Mr. LaGuardia he help me?

NEIL   He'll be here directly.

LOPEZ (*Reassuringly, to* ZAPPATELLA)   Mr. LaGuardia he help anybody.

MRS. POMERANTZ   I'm waiting first.

8

ZAPPATELLA (*To* NEIL) He help me—you sure?

NEIL Yes, I'm sure he'll help you—don't worry. (*Goes into private office and places a slip of paper on* FIORELLO's *desk*) Mr. LaGuardia will help you. (*He sings "On the Side of the Angels"*)

What a man!
What a job!
All these people
Who look to us for justice—
Trust us!

What a boss to work for
What a fine upstanding man he is
I'll follow in his footsteps
And do my level best
To earn a reputation like his.

I promise I'll proudly endure
The hardships I'll share
Working with this man
On the side of the angels.

My life will be selfless and pure
Like Upton Sinclair
Working with this man
On the side of the angels.

We're marching forward
Incorruptible, he and I
Battling with evil
Fighting till we drop
What a way to die!

So give me your tired, your poor,
And scoundrels, beware!
Here we stand in chorus
He and I and Morris
Standing firm, side by side,
On the side of the angels!
    (*He goes back to the switchboard*)

MORRIS (*At phone*) Shirley, how can I tell you when to put
the roast in? No, Shirley, only God and Mr. LaGuardia know
when I'll be there, and neither one tells me till the last minute.
I would ask him, but he hasn't come in yet. What a man is
right. (*He sings "On the Side of the Angels"*)
    What a job!
    What a man!
    What an office!
    That line of poor and friendless—
    Endless!

    Call the fire department
    There's another kitten up a tree
    Up goes Fiorello
    And everybody cheers
    And what does he use for a ladder?
    Me?

    Your life is an island of grief
    Surrounded by woe
    When you choose to work
    On the side of the angels.

My hours of leisure are brief
My wages are low
Working with this man
On the side of the angels.

That bench stays crowded
It's a regular wailing wall
Penniless and helpless
Ignorant and scared
He collects 'em all!

There's never a moment's relief
But this much I know
Each poor soul I see there
Could be me there
So I stay with this man
On the side of the angels!

NEIL (*At phone, covering mouthpiece*) Morris, will Mr. La
Guardia be willing to play cornet at the Saturday night dance
for the First Hibernian Sick and Benevolent Association?

MORRIS If they promise not to pay him. I think it will be okay.
Check with Miss Fischer.

DORA (*Enters*) Pardon me—

NEIL (*Into phone*) His secretary isn't here just now, but—

DORA Miss Fischer, please.

MRS. POMERANTZ I'm waiting first.

NEIL (*To* DORA)   One second—
   (*He turns back to the phone*)

DORA   It's terribly important. Somebody's in jail.
   (MARIE *enters from the outside, carrying a cornet. She is an attractive, wholesome, efficient girl*)

DORA (*Turning from* NEIL *and hurrying toward* MARIE)   Marie!
Thank Heaven!

MARIE   Dora! What's the matter?

DORA   Marie, please, you've got to get Mr. LaGuardia to help
us. They've arrested Thea.

MARIE   Come in here.

MRS. POMERANTZ   President Wilson's daughter!

MARIE (*She takes* DORA *into the inner office*)   Now for goodness'
sake, calm down. What happened?

DORA   Thea's our leader. She's the one got us to go out on strike
in the first place. She's the only one dares talk back to them.
And now they arrested her.

MARIE   For picketing? They can't do that.

DORA   Marie, not for picketing—for soliciting.

MARIE   For what?

DORA   Yes, soliciting. That crooked cop, he claims she was trying to pick up somebody.

MARIE   And she wasn't?

DORA No, she was just carrying a banner.

MARIE She wasn't—oh—flirting with anybody? Or wiggling or anything?
(*She twitches her hips just a trifle to illustrate*)

DORA No, no, she wasn't. She's not that kind at all. Somebody's just got to help us. You've got to help us—

MARIE Now, now—

DORA She's in jail, Marie, she's in jail.

MARIE Now please, Dora, don't get so excited. Cut it out. Gee whiz, Mr. LaGuardia will do something. I know he will. Now come on! You sit out here and just wait
(MARIE *takes* DORA *into the outer office. In the other room, the conversation now resumes*)

MR. ZAPPATELLA Look, I no want to go to jail.

MRS. POMERANTZ Who wants to go to jail?

MR. ZAPPATELLA My daughter she come home it's after eleven o'clock. She's out with a bad boy. I say: Don't go again or I hit. She go again. I hit. She call a policeman. He give me this summons.
(*The room freezes into silence as* FIORELLO *strides in through the outer door, wearing his famous sombrero, and, with scarcely a look at the people in the outer office, goes through to the inner office. He hangs up his hat and sits at the desk as though in the throes of great excitement. Meanwhile, after he has shut the door, the people in the outer office begin to murmur again. We don't notice*

them, however. We watch FIORELLO. *Suddenly he gives the desk a slap with the flat of his hand and jumps to his feet*)

FIORELLO (*With exalted decision*) Yes! (*He hurries back into the outer office. As he enters, all talking ceases abruptly. He looks around, spots* MARIE, *points a finger at her, and returns to his own office.* MARIE *jumps up, follows him in, and shuts the door*) Sit!

MARIE Mr. LaGuardia, something terrible has just happened.

FIORELLO (*An impatient wave of the hand*) Later.

MARIE My friend Dora, she's here about a girl they arrested for soliciting.

FIORELLO (*Preoccupied*) Marie, look. Ben Marino. The Republican leader of the Fourteenth District—you told me you knew him. What I'd like, Marie, I want you—(*Pause, then sharp*) Soliciting? A friend of yours?

MARIE Yes. But it's just a frame-up. They just do it to break the strike.

FIORELLO The strike?

MARIE The shirt-waist strike.

FIORELLO Marie, I'll take care of your friend's friend in just a moment. But first, I want you to arrange to introduce me to Ben Marino.

MARIE But—

FIORELLO   I just heard he's having trouble finding a candidate for Congress, and I want the nomination.

MARIE   (*Incredulous*) In the Fourteenth? Mr. LaGuardia, Tammany has that district sewed up. No Republican has ever gone to Congress from the Fourteenth. I can't believe you're serious.

FIORELLO   Try. Because I'm counting on you to introduce me to Ben. Why do you suppose I've spent all that time down at Silky Hetzel's Club in the Twelfth?

MARIE   I thought it was business.

FIORELLO   I was waiting for an opening. And now that I've found it, let's not waste any time. Bring your friend in. (*Sees cornet*) Oh, it's fixed. Good.
   (MARIE *goes to the outer office.* FIORELLO *blows a note on the cornet*)

MARIE   Dora—

MRS. POMERANTZ   (*Rising*) I'm waiting first.
   (DORA *follows* MARIE *into the inner office*)

DORA   Mr. LaGuardia, I can't tell you how—

FIORELLO   I've heard about that shirt-waist strike. First time women have been on the picket line.

DORA   They've arrested our leader. We've been out for six weeks and our money's about gone, and they arrested her, and the most awful part is it's for soliciting!

FIORELLO   And she wasn't?

DORA   No, sir. Just picketing. And Mr. Schirmer, the owner, he promised us if we'd work through the busy season we'd get a living wage, and then he broke his word. Honest, Mr. La Guardia, they treated us just terrible.

FIORELLO   My dear girl, I understand Mr. Schirmer and people like him. They'll stop at nothing. They murdered my father. (*He turns to* MARIE) Marie! Telephone Ben Marino and tell him we're on the way over.
(*He turns back to* DORA *as* MARIE *starts out of the room*)

DORA   They murdered your father?

FIORELLO   They did. (*Turns to* MARIE) Marie! Never mind. It's better just to walk in and surprise him. (*To* DORA, *as* MARIE *stops and turns back*) They poisoned him.

DORA   (*Aghast*)   The Nifty Shirt Waist Corporation?

FIORELLO   (*Impatient*)   No, the exploiters. That's the trouble with this younger generation. You don't grasp issues. You see the little things, and miss the big ones. They sold rotten food to the Army in the Spanish-American War—and my father died. (*To* MARIE) Send Morris in here. (*To* DORA, *as* MARIE *goes out to fetch* MORRIS) These same crooks will wear out your young lives working you twelve hours a day, then try to intimidate you by framing an innocent young girl and ruining her life—while they drive around in their great big shiny cars earned by the exploitation of children. (MORRIS *enters*) Morris, I want you to go right over to Ike Feeney's and arrange for a bail bond for a friend of this girl's.

MORRIS   Yes, sir.

16

FIORELLO (*To* DORA) Meantime, you go on back to strike headquarters and I'll meet you there.

DORA Thank you, Mr. LaGuardia.

MORRIS This way, miss.

FIORELLO (*To* DORA, *as he moves into outer office*) And don't be
afraid of Morris. Under that melon he calls a face, he's got a
kind heart. (FIORELLO *goes to the waiting group on the client's
bench*) All right, my friends. Who's first?
    (MARIE *remains in* FIORELLO's *office. Music starts for "On
    the Side of the Angels"*)

MR. ZAPPATELLA (*Singing*)
    I no want to go to jail

MR. LOPEZ (*Singing*)
    Tell me what I gotta do

MRS. POMERANTZ (*Singing*)
    I got such a lot of trouble and grief

ALL THREE
    I need relief
    That's why I come to you.
        (*The following is sung in counterpoint*)

MR. ZAPPATELLA	MARIE
I no want to go to jail	As long as he wants me, I know
MR. LOPEZ	
Tell me what I gotta do	I'll always be here

MRS. POMERANTZ

    I got such a lot of trouble and grief   Working with this man

ALL THREE

    I need relief   On the side of the angels.
    That's why I come to you.

MR. ZAPPATELLA   NEIL

    I'm in trouble with the law   Wherever he sends me, I'll go

MRS. POMERANTZ

    Don't know what it's all about   My duty is clear

LOPEZ

    I no got a lot of money to pay   Working with this man

ALL THREE

    People they say you help me out.   On the side of the angels.

MORRIS (*Solo, pointing to* DORA)

    Here's one more client
    Who's another financial gem
    I've yet to see the meek
    Inheriting the earth
    But we inherit them!

                (*In counterpoint*)

ALL THREE   MARIE, MORRIS, NEIL

    I was worried where to go   I know that he needs me,
    So I talk to all my friends   and so

FIORELLO!

Everybody say when you
    want the best
You go to Fiorello
Sure, they say you very
    smart
But more than that
They say you got a heart
Just like the angels.

I'll make my career
Working by his side
And proud to be allowed
    to
Side by side with this man
On the side of the angels.

Blackout

Scene Two

Place: The main room of the Ben Marino Association on West Third Street. Over a large round poker table covered with green baize, hangs a single electric bulb shielded by one of those porcelain shades that look like inverted ice-cream cones—white on the inside, green on the outside. In the background, through a haze of cigar smoke, we can see all the other recognizable symbols of a battered, musty political meeting house.

At rise: BEN'S POLITICAL HACKS *are seated around the table. They are playing five-card stud.* BEN MARINO *is not in the game. He paces back and forth.*

FIRST HACK   What do you say, Ben? You gonna take a hand?

BEN   Not now. Too much on my mind to play poker. Gotta settle on that damn candidate. (SEEDY MAN *enters*) Well, look who's here, my old friend Eddie Brown. How are you, Eddie?

SEEDY MAN (*Correcting him*) No, Harry.

BEN   Sure, Harry, isn't that what I said? Here—(*Takes a dollar from the pot*)—vote Republican—carfare.

SEEDY MAN   You bet, Mr. Marino. You can count on me.
    (*He exits*)

BEN   I doubt it.

20

THIRD HACK   That's your man, Ben. Run him.

BEN   May come to that yet. How about you? All you have to
do—

THIRD HACK   I know, I know—

FIFTH HACK   He's done it twice.

THIRD HACK   Nothing doing. This time get yourself a brand-
new sucker.

FIRST HACK (*To* BEN)   Sure you don't want to be dealt in?

BEN   No, go ahead.
(*They sing*)

FIRST HACK
King bets.

SECOND HACK
Cost you five.
Tony, up to you.

THIRD HACK
I'm in.

FOURTH HACK
So am I.

FIFTH HACK
Likewise.

FIRST HACK
Me, too.

BEN (*While the cards are being dealt*)
  Gentlemen, here we are, and one thing is clear:
  We gotta pick a candidate for Congress this year.

FIRST HACK
  Big ace.

SECOND HACK
  Ace bets.

THIRD HACK
  You'll pay—through the nose.

FOURTH HACK
  I'm in.

FIFTH HACK
  So am I.

FIRST HACK
  Likewise.

SECOND HACK
  Here goes.

FIRST HACK (*Examining the hands*)
  Possible straight,
  Possible flush,
  Nothing.

BEN
  Gentlemen, how about some names we can use?
  Some qualified Republican who's willing to lose?

SECOND HACK

How's about we should make Jack Riley the guy?

THIRD HACK

Which Riley are you thinking of? Jack B. or Jack Y.?

BEN

I say neither one,
I never even met 'em.

FOURTH HACK

I say:
When you got a pair of jacks,
Bet 'em!

ALL

Politics and poker
Politics and poker
Shuffle up the cards
And find the joker.
Neither game's for children,
Either game is rough.
Decisions, decisions, like:
Who to pick,
How to play,
What to bet,
When to call a bluff.

BEN (*Speaking*)   All right, now, fellas, politics or poker? Which
is more important?

FIRST HACK (*Singing*)
Pair of treys.

SECOND HACK
Bet 'em.

THIRD HACK
Little treys,
Good as gold.

FOURTH HACK
I'll stay.

FIFTH HACK
Raise you five.

FIRST HACK
I'll call.

SECOND HACK
I'll fold.

THIRD HACK
Raise you back.

FOURTH HACK
I think you're bluffin'.

THIRD HACK
Put your money where your mouth is.

BEN
Gentlemen, knock it off, and let's get this done.

FIFTH HACK
Try Michael Paniaschenkowitz, I'm certain he'd run.

24

BEN

Mike is out. I'm afraid he just wouldn't sell
Nobody likes a candidate whose name they can't spell.

FIRST HACK

How about Dave Zimmerman?

BEN

Davy's too bright.

SECOND HACK

What about Walt Gustafson?

BEN

Walt died last night.

THIRD HACK

How about Frank Monahan?

FOURTH HACK

What about George Gale?

BEN

Frank ain't a citizen, and
George is in jail.

FIFTH HACK

We could run Al Wallenstein.

BEN

He's only twenty-three.

FIRST HACK

What about Ed Peterson?

SECOND HACK
You idiot! That's me!

ALL
Politics and poker
Politics and poker
Playing for a pot
That's mediocre.
Politics and poker,
Running neck and neck.
If politics seems more
Predictable that's because usually you can stack the deck!
(*Enter* MARIE)

MARIE   Mr. Marino.

BEN   Well, if it isn't my old friend Miss Fischer. How are you, Miss Fischer?

MARIE   I came over because I want you to make the acquaintance of my boss, Mr. LaGuardia.

THIRD HACK   Huh!

BEN   Who?

THIRD HACK   That little wop with the big hat. (*Contemptuous*) Fiorello. You know him. He hangs around Silky Hetzel's in the Twelfth.
(FIORELLO *enters*)

FIORELLO   There are no little wops. Just big ones. As I'm ready and willing to demonstrate.

THIRD HACK   A modest guy, huh?

FIORELLO No, just a guy who happens to believe the way to beat Tammany is not—(*Reaches over, takes the* THIRD HACK'S *cards, and tosses them to center of table*)—by throwing in your cards. I came over to get this nomination.

FIRST HACK Is he kiddin'?

FIORELLO I never kid about serious issues, and I'm sitting on one right now that's big enough and hot enough to elect a Congressman from this district.

MARIE Ben, what have you got to lose?

BEN (*Dry*) Just another election, that's all.

FIORELLO You've been doing that long enough. Here's your chance to win for a change.

BEN With what?

FIORELLO The people of your own district. You think the men and women of the Fourteenth like the tenth-rate tinhorns they've had representing them in Congress for years?

BEN And you think—?

FIORELLO You give me the nomination, and I'll give you a Congressman.

BEN And if you don't?

FIORELLO (*Holds up his large sombrero*) See this hat?

BEN You might get indigestion.

27

FIORELLO   I'll take my chances on that. Do I get the nomination?

BEN (*Shrugging*)   Why not?

MARIE   Congratulations, Mr. Marino, you've just got yourself a wonderful candidate.

FIORELLO   Call me tomorrow and I'll show you how to lay out the campaign. Right now, I've got to go take care of the hot issue that's going to help elect me. Come on, Marie.
(FIORELLO *and* MARIE *exit*)

BEN (*Dry*)   Well, we got that settled.
(*The music starts. The players sing*)

THIRD HACK
Gimme three.

FOURTH HACK
Likewise.

FIFTH HACK
None for me. Standing pat.

FIRST HACK
Up to you.

SECOND HACK
I'm in.

THIRD HACK
I'm out.

FOURTH HACK
I'm flat.

FIFTH HACK (*Staring in direction taken by* FIORELLO)
    Wonder why any guy would lead with his chin
    Don't Fiorello realize he ain't gonna win?

SECOND HACK
    Ain't it obvious the
    Odds are too great?

BEN
    Some guys
    Always gotta try to fill an inside straight.
       (*He speaks*)
  If they didn't, where the hell would the fun be in the game?
       (BEN *joins the game*)

ALL
    Politics and poker
    Politics and poker
    Makes the av'rage guy
    A heavy smoker.
    Bless the nominee,
    And give him our regards,
    And watch while he learns
    That in poker and politics,
    Brother, you gotta have
    That slippery haphazardous commodity
    You gotta have the cards!

Blackout

Scene Three

Place: The street outside strike headquarters, which is in a store next to the Nifty Shirt Waist Factory.

At rise: DORA, NINA, BELLA, LENA, SOPHIE *and others are moving in a picket circle, holding their signs overhead. They have very little spirit. They are singing "Unfair."*

GIRLS
>Management's unfair
>Management's unfair
>Management is terribly unfair!
>>(*They are being taunted and jeered at by male* HECKLERS. *A policeman,* FLOYD, *is standing by, watching*)

FIRST HECKLER Go get pants!

THIRD HECKLER Go home, why don't you!

GIRLS (*Singing*)
>We've worked for a living all our lives
>We're dreadfully underpaid
>If you want to help your sisters and wives
>Your mothers and daughters
>Aid the lady strikers.

FIRST HECKLER (*Speaking*)
>Says you! You want the vote? Go on home!

THIRD HECKLER (*Speaking*)
>Woman's place is in the kitchen!

30

SECOND HECKLER (*Speaking*)
You wanna strike like men, you gotta dress like men!

NINA   Oh, shut up.

FIRST HECKLER   Go get pants!

NINA   We know why you're here—

DORA   Yes!

NINA   —insulting helpless women—'cause the company pays you to do it, that's why.

FIRST HECKLER   Woman's place is in the kitchen.

SOPHIE (*Tearful*)   How'd you like it if your sister had to work twelve hours a day, six days a week, for four dollars?

FIRST HECKLER   Go get pants!

SECOND HECKLER   Make a deal with you, girls! We'll teach you how to picket, if you teach us how to cook!
(*All* HECKLERS *laugh*)

NINA (*At breaking point*)   Somebody ought to teach you common decency!
(*She stumbles. She pauses to adjust the cardboard in the torn sole of her shoe*)

FLOYD (*Poking* NINA *with his night stick*)   Keep moving. No loitering allowed.

NINA   I'm not loitering. I've got a hole in my shoe.
(*She hops along on one foot*)

FLOYD   Keep moving, I tell you.
(*He pushes her*)

DORA   Hey, you stop that! What are you doing to that girl?

FLOYD   Another county heard from.

FIRST HECKLER   Wear pants!

FLOYD   And how does your big-mouthed girl friend like things
over at the jail?

DORA   You can ask her—'cause she'll be back here in a couple of
minutes. We got a lawyer now—and he got her out.

FLOYD   Stop all that lying and keep movin'.
(*He pushes* DORA)

DORA   You get your hands off me, you cossack! (HECKLERS *yell
tauntingly*) We got rights. Mr. LaGuardia says so.

FLOYD   And who, may I ask, is Mr. LaGuardia?

DORA   He's our lawyer.

NINA   Yeah—so there!

DORA   And we got a right to march—and you should be keeping
those goons from bothering us, instead of joining in with
them.
(HECKLERS *yell derisively*)

FIRST HECKLER   Wear pants!

32

FLOYD Now look. (*Walks along with* DORA) I got me duty to do.

DORA (*Hands him sign*) Hold this, will you, please?
(*She hops along, fixing the cardboard in her shoe*)

FLOYD What is this? Has everybody got holes in their shoes?

SOPHIE Sure we have.

NINA Where we going to get new shoes on our pay?

FLOYD Then why don't you be sensible and go back to work?

SECOND HECKLER Look!

THIRD HECKLER He's joined them!

FLOYD (*Becomes aware that he is carrying sign*) Here. What
do you think you're doing to me?
(*He thrusts the sign back into* DORA's *hands*)

SOPHIE We know why you want us to go back to work.

NINA 'Cause you're just a Tammany grafter like all the rest
of them.

FLOYD I don't want that kind of language.

NINA Then you leave us alone.

FIRST HECKLER Pull 'em in!

SECOND HECKLER Lock 'em up!

FIRST HECKLER Do your duty, Officer.

DORA   He doesn't dast to touch her.

FLOYD   Oh, I don't, eh?

NINA   No, you don't!

FLOYD   Well, you close that big mouth or I'll take you over to the station right now.

NINA   On what charge?

FLOYD   Solicitin'. I saw you wigglin'. I saw you trying to get those men over there. They'll testify.

DORA   All right, then, arrest me. Look, I'm wigglin'. (*She wiggles vigorously. The* HECKLERS *cheer*) Go ahead! Why don't you? And I'll get over there and we'll have a doctor's examination, and I guess that'll prove who's a liar. That'll prove whether I'm one of those women or not.

FLOYD   Oh, you're a pure thing, eh?

DORA   You're God damn right I am! (FIORELLO *and* MARIE *enter*) Oh, Mr. LaGuardia. This copper—this policeman—

FIORELLO   All right, all right. I'll take charge. I'd like a word with you, Officer.

FLOYD   And who are you?

FIORELLO   You'll learn in the course of the next few weeks. (*To* DORA) You girls got a headquarters?

DORA   In the store.

FIORELLO   All go in there.

DORA   And stop picketing?

FIORELLO   For the moment. We'll have a little meeting.

NINA   Stop picketing?

DORA   Do what he says. He's a lawyer. He knows what he's talking about.
(*The girls go out as* FIORELLO *continues the scene with* FLOYD)

FIORELLO   The name is Fiorello H. LaGuardia, and you better get it firmly in your mind because you're going to hear a good deal about me in the next few months.

FLOYD   I am, eh?

FIORELLO   If there is any further interference with these girls in the exercise of their constitutional rights, I'll slap a writ of interdictum on each and every perpetrator of such interference—beginning with you.

FLOYD   (*Suddenly uneasy*)   I'm just doing my duty, Counselor.

FIORELLO   I suggest you do it the way you promised under oath when you joined the force. I know what goes on behind the scenes, my friend. I know that this sweatshop and others like it have bought protection, and I intend to fight every one of them. I wouldn't like to see a nice intelligent fellow like you get caught in the middle.

FIRST HECKLER   Listen to him!

THIRD HECKLER   You gonna stand for that?

FLOYD (*Blustering at them to save face*)   Keep moving! Don't loiter! None of your lip! (*Crosses and waves the* HECKLERS *off the stage. Returns to* FIORELLO) I'll go back to the station house and report what you—what you just said about—about—you know.

FIORELLO   And if the Lieutenant has any difficulty understanding, I'll be glad to explain it to him, too. (*Hands* FLOYD *a card*) That's my office number. I answer calls from anybody.
      (FLOYD *goes*)

MARIE   I do admire you so.

FIORELLO   Well, I tell you, Marie. There's nothing like being right.

MARIE   I'll go back to the office and check on a few more bail bondsmen.

FIORELLO   Good.

MARIE   Good night.
      (*She starts out*)

FIORELLO   Marie. (*She turns*) Would you care to have dinner with me tonight?

MARIE   What?

FIORELLO   That is, if you're not busy?

MARIE   Oh no, I'm not.

FIORELLO Well?

MARIE Of course. Yes. Yes, I would.

FIORELLO I was going into an explanation—you know, the employer and his relations with people in the office—

MARIE Oh, Mr. LaGuardia, I understand.

FIORELLO But I have always wanted to know you better, Marie.

MARIE I accept your invitation.

FIORELLO Good. I'll pick you up at the office in about an hour. (MARIE *exits. Cheers are heard.* DORA *comes running in*) What's the matter?

DORA She's here! She's back!

FIORELLO Well, that's fine.
       (SOPHIE *runs in without shoes*)

SOPHIE She wants to see Mr.— She's back— Oh, excuse me. Thea—
       (SOPHIE *exits*)

FIORELLO (*Surprised as he stares offstage*) That girl? That's the girl they arrested?

DORA She's a model. She works in the front. But she's joined us.

FIORELLO That girl?

DORA She's our leader.
       (*Several girls enter*)

NINA   She's out!

SOPHIE   That'll show 'em!

DORA   Put one over on the cossacks that time!

NINA   Now we'll win!

GIRLS   We'll win!
(MORRIS *pushes through with* THEA)

FIORELLO   You did well, Morris.

MORRIS   She's out on Ike Feeney's five hundred dollars and her own recognizance. But I promised the judge that you'd be personally responsible. I'd have had her here sooner, but she insisted on washing her face.

FIORELLO   I can see that.

THEA   Thank you.

FIORELLO   Morris, you'd better line up a few more bondsmen. Then you can call Shirley and tell her to put the roast in the oven.

MORRIS (*Morose*)   Sure. Good night.
(*He exits*)

FIORELLO   Girls!

DORA   Yes, sir?

FIORELLO   You got any running water in there?
(*He points offstage*)

DORA   Yes, sir.

FIORELLO   Soap, too?

DORA   Uh-huh.

FIORELLO   All right. I don't want to see only one clean face. I want a lot of clean faces. In short, when you come back, I want you to look like girls again.

DORA (*Rubbing her dirty face*)   Yes, sir.

FIORELLO   And meantime I'll go over a few plans with this young lady.

DORA (*Introduces* THEA *to him as the girls exit*)   Miss Almerigatti.

FIORELLO   That's a good name. If you want to, you can call her Joan of Arc.

DORA   You bet.
      (*She exits*)

FIORELLO (*Indicating a battered soapbox*)   Won't you sit down, my dear young lady? I know what you've been through—even though we don't let them know.
      (THEA *sits. He walks up and down*)

THEA   Can we win?

FIORELLO   We can.

THEA   Somehow I believe you. But then I know, of course, that's not realistic. Lots of times I believe things can win and they don't come out that way.

FIORELLO You've got a just cause.

THEA Oh, I know that, but—

FIORELLO And you've got me. Believe in your cause and believe in me. This is my issue. As of today, I make it mine. For two reasons. Because I believe in your cause, and to be perfectly frank with you, because it will help me. A little thing like this is just what I need. Maybe it's the issue that will send me to the Congress of the United States of America. You think I'm talking a lot of nonsense, don't you? I'm the candidate from the Fourteenth District.

THEA Well, if we can help, I'm sure that—

FIORELLO You can—you can. Maybe you can help in more ways than one. You're an Italian girl—you're beautiful—you're smart. You can help me. One of the things I'm going to do is organize the Italian-Americans into political clubs.

THEA I should think it's about time that—

FIORELLO When people think of Italians, I want them to think of Michelangelo, Caruso, Garibaldi; not of Ponzi and the Mafia. Where you from?

THEA (*Rises proudly*) Trieste, an Italian city now being ground under the heel of the imperialistic Austrian invader.

FIORELLO Well! *Dunque siete veramente una Triestina?*

THEA (*Smiles with pleasure*) *Lo potete capire dal mio accento.*

FIORELLO When I was a kid, before I studied law, I was U. S. Consul in Fiume.

THEA   Fiume? Why, that's just across from—!

FIORELLO   Of course. I've been in Trieste many times.

THEA   Well, then, you know that isn't justice, is it? That's what I mean when you say we'll win. Trieste didn't win.

FIORELLO   You must be patient and believe in me.

THEA   I do, don't misunderstand me. (*Laughter offstage*) Listen! Look what you've done for us already, Mr. LaGuardia. That's the first laughter in days.

FIORELLO   And what you did, facing arrest—I don't forget that— that took courage. I admire it.

THEA   Do you really think we could win?

FIORELLO   I told you we could win this strike.

THEA   But do you know all about this situation?

FIORELLO   I don't know anything about it, but you're going to tell me.

THEA   There are so many problems. Are you going to have some time?

FIORELLO   Of course.

THEA   Right now, I mean?

FIORELLO   Certainly.

THEA   Could you perhaps take me to dinner?

FIORELLO (*Hesitates, then, slowly*)   Yes. Of course I could. That would be fine—just fine.

THEA   I'll wait for you, then.

FIORELLO   Good.
> (*The girls enter singing*)

GIRLS

> Management's unfair, management's unfair,
> Management is terribly unfair.

FIORELLO   Girls, girls—that's not the way to win.
> (*Sings*)
> You'd think that a human heart would break
> At such a display as this
> But warm-hearted men with money at stake
> Can turn into heartless
> Misbegotten misers
> Now a strike isn't played like tic-tac-toe
> And soft-spoken tactics just don't go
> Ladies you've got no choice
> You've got to holler and howl
> In your most unladylike voice
> Unfair!

GIRLS (*Timidly*)
> Unfair . . .

FIORELLO
> Louder—unfair!

GIRLS
> Unfair!

FIORELLO
Again—unfair!

GIRLS
Unfair!

FIORELLO
Good!
Let's put a stop
To the sweatshop
That's the disease we want to cure

Proudly we picket
The men who pick the pockets
Of the poor hard-working poor

While we stitch, stitch, stitch
Someone's getting rich
By the sweat of his sister's brow

GIRLS
Right!

FIORELLO
Let's fix the wagon
Of this gold-hungry dragon
Let's trim the fat
From this sacred cow!
You've got to howl at the top of your voice

GIRLS
Unfair!

FIORELLO
Holler and howl at the top of your voice

GIRLS
> Unfair!

FIORELLO
> Keep yelling foul at the top of your voice

GIRLS
> Unfair!

> Let's put a stop
> To the sweatshop
> Let's end the evil of the age

> Fight to the finish
> To win the war we're waging
> For a decent living wage

> Must we sew, and sew
> Solely to survive
> So some low so-and-so
> Can thrive?
> No!
> He'll fry in Hades
> If it's up to the ladies
> Waistmaker's union
> Local twenty-five!
> (*Shouting*)
> Unfair! Unfair! Unfair! Unfair!
> (*All exit left*)

Blackout

Scene Four

FIORELLO'S *office immediately following the preceding scene.* MORRIS *is on the phone in the outer office;* MARIE *is on the phone in the inner office.*

MARIE (*Into phone*)   It's only just in case, Mr. Lamberti.

MORRIS (*Into phone*)   Ike Feeney went to five hundred for one of them, but she was the leader. For the others, in case they're arrested, it won't be more than two fifty—three hundred top. They're very small girls. (*Pause*) Thanks, George.
(*He hangs up and makes a note on his pad*)

MARIE (*Into phone*)   That's very nice of you, Mr. Lamberti. Mr. LaGuardia will appreciate it.
(*She hangs up and makes a note on her pad*)

MORRIS (*Calls to her*)   How do we stand?

MARIE (*Examining her list*)   It's all right.

MORRIS   Then we're okay as long as they don't get arrested for anything worse than soliciting. (*The phone rings.* MORRIS *speaks into phone*) Hello? Yes, she is. Just a moment, Mr. La Guardia. (*To* MARIE) It's for you.
(MARIE *comes to him*)

MARIE (*Eager, into phone*)   Hello? (*Pause*) Yes, Mr. LaGuardia? (*Pause*) Mr. LaGuardia, is something wrong? (*Pause*)

45

Yes. (*Pause*) No, no, that's all right. I understand. (*Pause. Then, with forced brightness*) No, I don't mind. (*Pause*) Of course. Good night, Mr. LaGuardia.

(*She hangs up slowly*)

MORRIS (*Quiet*)   Anything wrong?

MARIE (*Quick*)   No, my list is complete.

MORRIS   You know what I mean. What's the matter?

MARIE   Nothing. (*Suddenly angry*) I'm just a damn fool, that's all.

MORRIS   There's no law against that.

MARIE   Well, there ought to be.

MORRIS   Now . . . now.

MARIE   I'd like to make the laws.

MORRIS   I bet they'd be good.

MARIE   Oh, would they! Would they! You bet they would. Here —take a law—write this down.
(*She sings "Marie's Law"*)
    My law shall state
    To whom it may concern

MORRIS (*Singing*)
    Your law shall state
    To whom it may concern

MARIE

>When a lady loves a gentleman
>He must love her in return

MORRIS

>Loves a gentleman he must love her in re . . .

MARIE

>In re, my law
>Ad hoc, to wit, to woo

MORRIS

>In re, your law
>Ad hoc, to wit, to woo

MARIE

>When a lady feels affectionate
>Then the man must follow through

MORRIS

>Feels affectionate then the man must follow . . .

MARIE

>Here's another law we women'll
>Do our best to legislate
>It shall be completely criminal
>For a man to break a date
>Each offender shall be rapidly
>Thrown in jail where he belongs
>Thus we'll right our bill of wrongs
>
>My law is what
>The world is waiting for

MORRIS

> Your law is what
> The world is waiting for

MARIE

> Every unrequited lover will be grateful when it
> Meets the full approval of the House and Senate
> Such enthusiasm as you never saw
> Will greet my lovely law.
>
> In re, my law
> It should be understood

MORRIS

> In re, your law
> It should be understood

MARIE

> With the help of women everywhere
> We shall outlaw bach'lorhood

MORRIS

> Women everywhere you shall outlaw bach'lorhood . . .

MARIE

> What's more . . . in lieu

MORRIS

> Marie, before you're through
> I've got some things
> I'd like to say. If you
> Have got to outlaw anything
> You should outlaw in-laws, too.

Toward left, smoking a cigar and wearing a derby, Howard Da Silva
as BEN MARINO. Immediately to his right, Patricia Wilson, Tom Bosley,
Ellen Hanley, and Nathaniel Frey, as MARIE, FIORELLO, THEA, and MORRIS

MARIE
 I'm concerned with what the man must do

 Every girl shall have a honeymoon
 Which shall last at least a year
 During which aforesaid honeymoon
 Every care shall disappear
 Ipso facto, let the government
 Get the bride and groom alone
 After that they're on their own.

 Whereas

MORRIS
 Whereat

MARIE
 Hereby

MORRIS
 Hereof

MARIE
 Therein

MORRIS
 They're out and furthermore

MARIE
 My law

MORRIS
 Your law

MARIE
>   Is what

MORRIS
>   Is what

MARIE
>   The world

MORRIS
>   The world is waiting for

MARIE
>   We are going to rid the country
>   Of contempt of courtship

MORRIS
>   Legally replacing it
>   With davenportship

BOTH
>   Such enthusiasm as you never saw
>   Will greet (my/your) lovely law.

Blackout

Scene Five

Place: A street corner.

At rise: Enter NEIL, BEN MARINO *and* MIKE, *carrying a stepladder platform.*

BEN (*To* NEIL, *as they move across the stage*)   Well, this is a good time to break the ice, kid. Maybe you'll become a great orator. You'll have a crowd around you in no time. All right, this way to the LaGuardia rally.

NEIL (*Mounting stepladder*)   And I'm going to ask you to vote for Fiorello H. LaGuardia. (NEIL *stands on the stepladder, stage left, addressing a small crowd. A couple of the Republican politicians are standing near the ladder.* DORA *and some of the girl strikers are in the crowd.* FLOYD *is off at one side, watching. Later he works his way across to talk to* DORA) I want to ask you to consider not only the issues but the man. I know this man and he is just great—that's what I'm telling you—he's just great. If you knew him as I do, you'd realize what a great thing it would be to have such a great man represent you in Congress. Now he'll be here a little later to talk to you himself, but in the meantime, here's another speaker who wants to address you.

(*The politicians lead a little applause.* NEIL *gets down to make way for* THEA, *who is helped up the ladder. While this is going on,* FLOYD *addresses* DORA)

51

FLOYD Now, miss, you mustn't hold that against me. Anyhow, I hear you won the strike.

DORA Yes—we did.

FLOYD (*Shakes hands*) Congratulations. I'm glad.

THEA (*On platform*) I'm a working girl. I model for the Nifty Shirt Waist Company. And I see that some of you are working people, too. (*Laughter and applause*) The girls in that factory were working twelve hours a day for four dollars a week. They were promised a living wage; they didn't get it; they struck. Who would help us? Nobody. Until one man, one man who hates injustice and tyranny of any type, took up our cause, and got us our rights, and that's why I'm for him. And here he is to talk to you himself—Fiorello H. LaGuardia.

> (*They help her down.* FIORELLO *comes in followed by* MARIE. *He mounts the ladder*)

FIORELLO Friends, I want each and every one of you to take a long deep breath! Like this! (*He illustrates*) You know what that smell is? Tammany! They've been stinking up this district long enough. It's time to get the garbage off the doorsteps, and I've got the shovel to do it with. Your vote! Put that pencil cross next to the name of Fiorello H. LaGuardia! L-A-G-U-A-R-D-I-A!
> (*He sings*)
> Now here's another name
> T-A-M-M-A-N-Y, what's that?

VOICE (*Speaking*) Tammany?

FIORELLO (*Speaking*) Wrong!
> (*Singing*)

The answer's tyranny
Tammany spells tyranny
Like r-a-t spells rat!

Now there's a double "M" in Tammany
And a double "L" in gall
Just like the double-dealing
Double-crossing
Double-talking
Double-dyed duplicity
Of Tammany Hall!

But you can change it all
Go use the ballot box
And cast your spell come next election day
The name's LaGuardia
L-A-G-U-A-R-D-I-A!

CROWD

L-A-G-U-A-R-D-I-A!
(*The lights go down quickly and come up at stage right, where an Italian audience is being addressed by* THEA)

THEA . . . and who is against tyranny of every type, and who believes that Trieste should go back to the Italian people— (*Cheers*) And here he is, Fiorello LaGuardia!
(*Cheers. She gets down and* FIORELLO *mounts the ladder.* DORA *comes in accompanied by* FLOYD)

FIORELLO (*In Italian*) *Amici!*

A MAN *Amici!*

FIORELLO *Trieste deve esser libera e noi dobbiamo esser liberi.*
(*The crowd cheers*)

53

FIORELLO *Attenti!*

ANOTHER MAN *Attenti!*

FIORELLO (*He sings the song in Italian. The lyrics spelled phonetically*)
> *Kees*-tuh vay *vaw*-lyoh *dee*
> Ah-tee-tee-eh-en-tee-ee, ah tahm-mah-*nee*
>
> Kay *fays* see vay vaw *fah*
> Vay-*nee*-tay *toot*-tee *kwahn*-tee toot-tee
> Kwahn-tee ahk-*kah, noon fah*-tay-vay'ngahn-*nah!*

CHORUS (*Singing*)
> Ah tahm-mah-nee
> Bravo, LaGuardia, bravo!
> (*The lights go down and come up again at stage left, where another part of the city is indicated.* MORRIS *is on a platform addressing a crowd, many of whom are Jewish*)

MORRIS . . . and a fearless man and an honest man—a man who will look after your interests.

HECKLER Look after the Italian interest, you mean!

MORRIS I mean all interests without fear or favor. And my name is not King Victor Emmanuel—it's Morris Cohen!

WOMAN Moisha Cohen!
> (*Laughter and applause*)

MORRIS And here he comes now—he'll tell you himself.
> (DORA *and* FLOYD *appear at the edge of the crowd*)

DORA (*Smiling at* FLOYD) It's very nice of you to walk me over.
> (FIORELLO *is on the ladder. Applause*)

FIORELLO   Friends—I've just come from Mulberry Street.

HECKLER   Little Italy, huh? You're always talking about your Italian background. I hear you're half Jewish. How come you never brag about your Jewish background?

FIORELLO   I figure if a man is only half Jewish it isn't enough to brag about.
>   (FIORELLO *sings a Yiddish version of the song. The lyrics are spelled phonetically*)
>   Ich bin LaGvardia

MRS. POMERANTZ (*Speaking*)   Mr. LaGuardia!

FIORELLO
>   Doss is La-med A-leph Gim-mel A-leph Raysh
>   Doll-ed yood eyen dee far-guess doss nischt
>   Ich zug tsu eye-ich, Tammany is nisht kosher
>   Hahb doss in zinnen
>   Und heatzich foon zay!

CHORUS
>   La-med A-leph Gim-mel A-leph Raysh Doll-ed
>   Yood eyen meer veln doss nisht far-guessen
>   La-med A-leph Gim-mel A-leph Raysh Doll-ed
>   Yood eyen meer veln doss nisht far-guessen.
>   (*The crowd erupts in a wildly enthusiastic street dance into which are drawn* FIORELLO, THEA, *and* MORRIS)

CHORUS (*Singing. Exultant*)
>   The name's LaGuardia
>   L-A-G-U-A-R-D-I-A!

Blackout

SCENE SIX

BEN MARINO *and his political hacks come straggling out on stage. They carry newspapers. They look dazed. They sing "The Bum Won."*

BEN (*Singing*)
Even without our help
Look at the way he won
Everyone sold him short!

FIRST HACK (*Speaking*)   You think they'll ask for a recount?

BEN (*Singing*)
We got a winner
But what good is that to us?
Not if he doesn't feel
Grateful for our support

FIRST HACK (*Speaking*)   You mean no patronage, huh, Ben?

BEN
I gotta talk to him.

SECOND HACK (*Singing*)
Someone pinch me
Maybe this is just a beautiful dream
I'm in a bad state of shock

SECOND *and* THIRD HACK (*Singing*)
I'd like to know just how the hell it happened

56

What we did right
Fellas, the whole thing is cockeyed.

FIRST, FOURTH *and* FIFTH HACK
We got a winner at last
We got a star which is in the ascendant

BEN
If he feels that we sloughed him off
He could become, God forbid, independent.

SIXTH HACK
Who'd ever guess that the people would go
To the polls and elect a fanatic?
People can do what they want to
But I got a feeling it ain't democratic

BEN
This is a guy that is gonna go further
Than anyone ever suspected

SIXTH HACK
Yesterday morning I wrote him a note
That I'm sorry he wasn't elected!
(*In counterpoint*)

BEN
Even without our help
Look at the way he won
Everyone sold him short
We got a winner
But what good is that to us
Not if he doesn't feel
Grateful for our support

SECOND *and* THIRD HACKS
Someone pinch me
Maybe this is just a beautiful dream
I'm in a bad state of shock
I'd like to know just how the hell it happened
What we did right
Fellas, the whole thing is cockeyed

FIRST, FOURTH *and* FIFTH HACKS

We got a winner at last
We got a star which is in
the ascendant

If he feels that we
sloughed him off
He could become, God
forbid, independent.

SIXTH HACK

Who'd ever guess that the
people would go
To the polls and elect a
fanatic?
People can do what they
want to
But I got a feeling it ain't
democratic
This is a guy that is gonna
go further
Than anyone ever suspect-
ed.
Yesterday morning I
wrote him a note . . .

BEN

I had to go take an amateur from the ranks
Make him the nominee
What does he do? He wins!

FIRST HACK (*Speaking*)   Kind of makes you believe in miracles,
huh, Ben?

SIXTH *and* FOURTH HACKS

The bum won

SECOND *and* THIRD HACKS

The bum won

BEN (*Mournful*)

God forbid, independent!

FIORELLO!

FIRST *and* FIFTH HACKS
> We gotta talk to him.
> (*They begin to straggle off listlessly, repeating lines from "The Bum Won" until they are offstage*)

Blackout

Scene Seven

Place: A dreary Greenwich Village tenement roof with one cheerful spot—a table with a bright cloth and tea things. Two hatboxes are at one side.

At rise: DORA, *in a neat dress, sits at the table. She is pouring tea —a second cup.* FLOYD, *his back to us, is looking over the parapet toward the street.*

FLOYD (*Calls down*) You ain't in no rush. Sure it's important. Ten minutes. (*Turns and comes to her. His coat is unbuttoned*) Riley's a good egg—he's in no hurry.
  (*He tries to kiss her*)

DORA Oh, Floyd—not in the middle of the day.

FLOYD My feelings don't watch the clock. I get thinking of that kiss you gave me last night and then I can't think of nothing else.

DORA Floyd, think of duty. You got to go to work. Besides, Marie is coming over.

FLOYD Which Marie—the dopey one?

DORA Floyd, you're going to make me very angry.

FLOYD I love you when you're angry.
  (*He chases her*)

60

DORA Floyd—not now, you brute! (*Pounds his chest with her fists*) You cossack!

FLOYD (*Releases her*) Okay. That's one you owe me. What's that Marie want of you anyway?

DORA She wants to borrow a hat. She's going to Washington.

FLOYD Down to see the little wop, huh? Boy, is that big mouth getting himself in trouble down there.

DORA He is, Floyd?

FLOYD Is he? He's trying to get us into war. Didn't you read the papers?

DORA Not lately.

FLOYD Me neither. But I listen. I hear things. Oh, they hate him —his own district—they hate him. He couldn't get elected again. Not to nothing.

DORA Mr. LaGuardia won our strike, that's all I know.

FLOYD Huh!

DORA And he got to Congress, didn't he?

FLOYD That's another thing. They was talkin' about it over to the Wigwam. How come they let that little squirt walk off with the Fourteenth District right from under their noses? And I give my opinion: overconfidence, I says. And one of the very important guys there, he says to me: Floyd McDuff, you're only walking a beat now, but mark my words, he says, one of these days I expect you to be a sergeant, he says. And maybe even higher, he says.

DORA   I bet you will, too. I believe in you, Floyd.

FLOYD   And you know what he says? He says—with a kind of a wink, you know—he says: You may not be the smartest guy on the force, but you're loyal.

DORA   And what did you say to him?

FLOYD   I says, Judge, thank you.

DORA   That was real smart.
(*A knock.* MARIE *pokes her head out through stair door*)

DORA   Marie! I'm so glad to see you.

DORA   Marie! I'm so glad to see you.
(*Runs to embrace her*)

FLOYD   Ah, hello there, Marie. How are you?

MARIE   Fine.

DORA   Come on out.

FLOYD   Well, my sidekick is waiting for me down there. Good-bye, Marie.

MARIE   Good-bye.

FLOYD   See you tonight, Dora. Thanks for the tea—(*He gives her a meaningful bump with his hip*) and the sugar.
(*He laughs and hurries out, buttoning his tunic*)

MARIE   Your new admirer seems in high spirits.

DORA   Sure. He's very good-natured. Want some tea?

MARIE   No, thanks. I just stopped down at the corner and had a Moxie.

DORA   Marie, you shouldn't drink Moxie.

MARIE   No? Why not?

DORA   Didn't you know that Moxie is bad for the teeth?

MARIE   Moxie?

DORA   Floyd says if you put an ordinary molar in a glass of Moxie, and you keep it there overnight, in the morning you'll find the tooth is completely disappeared.

MARIE   Floyd told you that?

DORA   Yes.

MARIE   Well, as long as you're happy, that's the main thing.

DORA   Oh, I am, I'm happy. But, Marie—I'm miserable, too!

MARIE   You don't act it.

DORA   Life is so complicated.
  (*She sings "I Love a Cop"*)
  I love a cop
  I love a cop
  What a situation; ain't it awful?

Life is really grim . . .
I can only say that it's unlawful
How I feel towards him . . .

I love a cop
I love a cop
If I introduce him as my steady
Down at where I work,
I can hear the rumor spread already
Dora's gone beserk!

Then there's Thea . . . Oh, how gruesome!
Can you see me introduce 'em?
"You remember her—
She detested you."
"You remember him,
He arrested you!"

I'm so confused
I'm so confused
If I loved a dentist or a doctor
I'd be up on top
But I . . . love . . . a cop!

I love a cop
I love a cop
Though it wasn't easy to accept him
Now I think he's sweet
You should hear him tell the way I swept him
Off his big flat feet.

I love a cop
I love a cop
I can see his drawbacks clear as crystal

Still I testify
Once you take away his club and pistol
Floyd won't hurt a fly.

Floyd's ambitious and he's forceful
Energetic and resourceful
I can see how far
This will carry him
If he'd get an honest job
I would marry him.

That's how it is
He's mine . . . I'm his
Little did I know when Floyd first kissed me
And I whispered, "Stop!"
You can't . . . stop . . . a cop!
    (*Speaking*)   Ah, Marie, it's so wonderful for two people
to be in love.

MARIE   Yes, even for one people.

DORA   What?

MARIE   Nothing.

DORA   Is that why you're going to Washington? Did Mr. La
Guardia invite you?

MARIE   No, Ben Marino.

DORA   Is he your latest?

MARIE   It's business, Dora, just business.

DORA (*Grinning*)   Monkey business.

MARIE   Oh, Dora, don't be so romantic.

DORA   (*Runs to the hatboxes*)   Well, I brought my two best hats up. See—put this on—it'll knock him dead.

MARIE   (*Puts on hat*)   How do I look?

DORA   I don't know. Take a look.

MARIE   (*Examines herself in a mirror*)   I'll tell you the truth, Dora, I'm going because Mr. Marino thinks I have influence. He thinks I can tell Mr. LaGuardia what to say in Congress— which is utterly ridiculous. But oh, well, at least I'll get a chance to see Washington.

DORA   You better take a good look, Marie, because Floyd says if Mr. LaGuardia doesn't stop trying to send American boys over there to fight for those foreigners—Floyd says he'll never get elected again.

MARIE   Well, at least that would keep him in New York.

DORA   (*Grinning*)   I knew it! I can see right through you. I knew it!

MARIE   Thank you for the hat. Thanks loads. Good-bye.
(*She exits.* DORA *dances a wistful, impish, wordless refrain to "I Love a Cop"*)

Blackout

66

Scene Eight

Place: LaGuardia's office in the House Office Building in Washington.

At rise: FIORELLO *sits at his desk, working. He is writing a speech. He puts his glasses on, writes a few words, stops, takes the glasses off, gestures with them, puts them back on, mutters a few phrases inaudibly. He even rises at one point to practice a high spot in his oration.*

The buzzer sounds. FIORELLO *lifts receiver of desk box and listens.*

FIORELLO (*Into box*)   Send the senator in, and let me know the minute the Ben Marino party gets here. (*He hangs up, pushes the glasses up on his forehead, and sits waiting. A* SENATOR *is ushered in. He is the old-school conservative type—ponderous and benign.* FIORELLO *rises and shakes his hand*) Senator.

SENATOR   Congressman. Thank you for letting me intrude upon you at this time. I understand you're busy.

FIORELLO   Trying to earn my money.

SENATOR   Congressman, I've often wanted to have a chance to exchange ideas with you. And I do hope such an opportunity develops before long.

FIORELLO   Thank you, Senator.

SENATOR   Right now I come in here upon a matter which concerns you and me both, because it concerns our party. I've been told that you're planning to make a speech.

FIORELLO   That is correct.

SENATOR   You've been very active in things in Washington, Congressman LaGuardia, and that's as it should be. But as you undoubtedly know, there's an unwritten law, a piece of cherished etiquette, I might say, that a freshman member does not speak on the floor of the House during his first term.

FIORELLO   Yes, I've heard about that. It seems ridiculous, doesn't it?

SENATOR   You don't believe that tradition has its value, Congressman?

FIORELLO   Not very much, I guess.

SENATOR   But you could be wrong, of course.

FIORELLO (*Casual*)   That's possible.

SENATOR   And you could be wrong in this rash support you are proposing to give to the Draft Act.

FIORELLO (*Firm*)   Only I'm not. When the Congressman from Milwaukee takes the floor again, I shall take the floor. The pacifists are poisoning the thought of the country. They have to be answered. Breaking a rule of etiquette is a small, small price for the House to pay.

SENATOR   Only the House won't pay, my dear LaGuardia—you will pay.

68

FIORELLO   That's all right with me. I can't remain quiet any
longer. Did you read his speech yesterday? When you boil
away all the phony blubber, you find what this genius has
been telling us is that we can win this war without men. Let
the Allies do the fighting, he says. All we have to do is write a
few checks. And look at our allies. France? Senator, you know
what a shirt looks like when it's made one trip to the laundry
too many? (*He snatches up a shirt from the desk, and pulls it
on over his head. The material is so threadbare, it tears*) That's
France. Completely worn out. Who else? England? Ever
have a tooth yanked, Senator? The dentist fills the hole with a
fake. You have enough of them yanked, you get enough fakes
as replacements, and pretty soon you've got a complete set of
china choppers. (*Pulls a pair of false teeth from his coat
pocket*) They look all right, but there's damned little bite in
them. And after four years of replacements, that's what the
British Army is like today—damned little bite in it. Italy?
One pork chop, Senator. (*Snatches up a raw pork chop and
brandishes it under the* SENATOR's *nose*) That's the daily food
ration of the average Italian soldier.

SENATOR   All that may be very true, sir, but the fact remains—

FIORELLO   When you're in a war, Senator, there are no buts.
You have only two choices. You can win, or you can lose. If
we depend on France—(*Tugs at the torn shirt he is wearing*)
—on England—(*Snatches up the false teeth and drops them
on the desk*)—on Italy—(*Snatches the pork chop and slaps it
down on the desk*)—we sure as hell won't win this one!

SENATOR   Now, wait one minute, sir!

FIORELLO   We can't spare that minute, Senator. We can't wait.
Because we're in terrible danger. We've got to prepare before

69

it's too late. We've got to get the men—American men—to save our American lives!

SENATOR Please, sir—

FIORELLO And there's only one fair and honest and democratic way to get those men—a Draft Act! (*The intercom buzzes. He snatches up receiver and speaks into the box*) Yes? Good. (*Hangs up, then speaks to the* SENATOR) Excuse me. (*Hurries out, leaving the door open. Offstage voices are heard.* FIORELLO *says,* "*Welcome, welcome,*" *to which* BEN MARINO *replies,* "*Good to see you, Congressman.*" *The* SENATOR *fumes, then starts out as* FIORELLO *re-enters*) Senator—I'm sorry.

SENATOR (*Pompous*) I don't believe there is anything else we can discuss at this moment. Thank you very much.
(*He exits*)

FIORELLO Thank you. (*Turning toward the open door*) Come in—come in. (MARIE *and* BEN *enter*) Well, I told you I'd be here and here I am. How do you like it?
(BEN *and* MARIE *stare at him*)

MARIE Lovely.
(*She giggles*)

FIORELLO What's the matter?

MARIE Is that what the well-dressed Congressman wears?

FIORELLO (*Looks down at himself*) Oh! Oh, this. It's to illustrate a point. I'm using it in my speech tomorrow.
(*He takes off the shirt*)

BEN (*Incredulous*) You're going to wear that thing down on the floor of the House?

FIORELLO Why not?

BEN (*Dry, to* MARIE) Maybe we got here just in time.

FIORELLO In time for what, Ben?

BEN Marie—talk to him.

FIORELLO Talk to me about what?

MARIE We all want you to be successful.

FIORELLO Never mind about that. Talk to me about what?

MARIE The Draft Act.

FIORELLO I see.

MARIE Up in the Fourteenth the people are—they're terribly upset by the—by the way you—they're angry, Mr. LaGuardia, because you're backing the Draft Act.

FIORELLO I'm sorry about that. I must have fallen down on the job of keeping them informed. I thought I'd explained the issue clearly. I thought they understood what's at stake.

MARIE Oh, they do, Mr. LaGuardia. They understand the issue.

FIORELLO Then how can they be angry?

MARIE They—you see, they don't care about the issue. They just want to keep their boys at home.

FIORELLO So do I.

BEN (*An angry outburst*) If you're telling the truth, if you really want to keep the boys at home, why do you want to go yelling your head off down there on the floor of the House? Why all this let's pass this Draft Act right away in a hurry this minute fast or we're all dead ducks?

FIORELLO (*Very quiet*) Because when the people of the Fourteenth voted for me, and sent me down here, they changed me a little. They may not have known they were doing it—they may not even be aware they've done it—but they made me a little different from themselves. I can no longer think the way they think, as a single individual, a father or a mother thinking about a son. I have to think about the whole country, all the people in it, what's best for all of them. I'm not a guy hanging around a political club any more, Ben. I'm a Congressman now.

BEN (*Sore*) I wonder how your thinking would go if this Draft Act applied not only to people but also to Congressmen?

FIORELLO (*Quiet*) You can stop wondering about that. I enlisted this morning.

Blackout

Scene Nine

Place: A street.

At rise: Several soldiers walk across the stage. They meet NEIL *as he enters.*

FIRST SOLDIER It's at the Ben Marino club. They got the yard all fixed up.

SECOND SOLDIER Hi, Neil. Comin' to the party?

NEIL Sure. First I gotta pick up my girl. (*A drunk enters carrying a sign: "Good-bye,* FIORELLO." NEIL *laughs*) There's somebody who's going, all right.
(*The drunk staggers off.* DORA *and* FLOYD *enter.* FLOYD *is in civilian clothes*)

NEIL Hello, Dora. How are you, Mr. McDuff?
(*The soldiers and* NEIL *exit.* DORA *and* FLOYD *start across the stage. Then* FLOYD *stops suddenly*)

FLOYD (*Sullen*) Listen, Dora, I'm not going.

DORA Now, Floyd, have we got to go all through that again?

FLOYD When I see those guys in uniform . . .

DORA Well, it's not your fault. You tried. You can't help it if you've got flat feet.

73

FLOYD I know what they say about me. I can see them looking at me.

DORA Floyd, I've got to go to Mr. LaGuardia's farewell party, and I couldn't have any fun without you. I'd just be miserable. Now please come with me. I'm so proud of you. You're so handsome, and you're going up in the world.

FLOYD Well, maybe I am.

DORA Oh, I know you are.

FLOYD I'm started, ain't I?

DORA That's what I say. And now you got this job in the sewer department, who knows where it will all end? Floyd, if you just go to the party and be nice—then afterward—tonight—
    (*She kisses him*)

FLOYD (*Hoarse, as he comes up out of the kiss*) What?

DORA (*Reprises "I Love a Cop"*)
    I love a cop
    I love a cop
    I will not allow my friends to taunt you
    Honest, Floyd, that's true
    Even if your Uncle Sam don't want you
    Mister, I sure do!

    I know why they won't enlist you
    It's because they never kissed you
    Even though your feet are a wee bit flat
    Maybe I can help you forget all that.

    Now, Floyd Mc "D",
    You come with me

Little did I know when I first met you
One day I'd be yours
And you'd . . . be . . . in sewers!
> (*Enter* SOLDIERS *and* GIRLS. DORA *pantomimes a request for
> their help in persuading* FLOYD)

DORA, SOLDIERS, GIRLS (*Singing*)
We love a cop
We love a cop
> (*The soldiers seize* FLOYD *and start dragging him to the
> party*)

FLOYD (*Singing*)
I don't wanna argue with you doughboys
Let's get one thing clear
Either you decide to let me go, boys,
Or we'll have a private war right here.
> (*He shakes himself free but is promptly seized by the
> girls*)

GIRLS
We know you're a patriot, Floyd
In a uniform or not, Floyd
No one thinks of you as an also-ran
We prefer to think you're a plain-clothes man

ALL
We love a cop
We love a cop
Come along and join our friendly send-off
You have stalled enough
So lead . . . on . . . McDuff!
> (*They exit with* FLOYD)

Blackout

Scene Ten

Place: The main room of the Ben Marino Association on West Third Street.

At rise: Music and cheers are heard from the yard, which is shut off, so that only the small set in the center of the stage is exposed. MARIE *is sitting at card table. She is affected by the sadness of* FIORELLO's *departure.*

MORRIS *stands at the door, looking out at crowd dancing in the yard. The dancing stops; the crowd applauds.*

MORRIS   They sure are giving him a great send-off.

MARIE   Yes.
(*She lowers her face to cover her quivering lip*)

MORRIS (*Turns*)   What's the matter, Marie?

MARIE (*Very small voice*)   What if I never see him again?

MORRIS (*Touches her shoulder reassuringly*)   You will.

MARIE   I'm sorry, Morris.

MORRIS   They can't kill him.

MARIE   Bullets can kill anybody.

MORRIS   No, not him.

FIORELLO (*His voice is heard out in the yard*) Let's get out of it for a couple of seconds. (FIORELLO *and* THEA *come in.* FIORELLO *wears a flier's uniform;* THEA, *a party dress*) Hello, you two.

MORRIS Great turnout, Mr. LaGuardia.

THEA Isn't it wonderful? Everybody, just everybody! Aren't you proud, Marie?

MARIE (*Managing to control her voice*) Oh, yes.
(*She goes out*)

FIORELLO Where is she going?

MORRIS Those papers, you know, before you go. I'll check on it.
(*He goes out after her*)

THEA Dear Marie, she's so upset about your going away.

FIORELLO I don't want her to be. I told her I was going to come back.

THEA I know you will.

FIORELLO Thea—this is our last chance to talk.

THEA No, it isn't. We'll talk when you come back.

FIORELLO You know what's going to happen when I come back, don't you?

THEA You're going to run for President.

FIORELLO Better yet—I'm going to marry you.

THEA Do we have to discuss marriage?

FIORELLO Thea—you're in my thoughts constantly. Now, I'm not an idiot. And I know you have other men who are in love with you—as I am. So I want to have you tell me now—before I go away—what's the score? That's what I want to know—what's the score?

THEA I do admire you so much—you know that—and I respect you. But is that enough for marriage?

FIORELLO I thought we were very close, Thea.

THEA Oh, yes. We have been—and when you helped us win our strike, and when I helped you win your seat in Congress—those were wonderful days.

FIORELLO We'll have more of them.

THEA I'm so confused. I've been asking a little advice.

FIORELLO If you want advice, you come to me.

THEA I asked a friend of mine, Father O'Rourke. I asked him did he think it a good idea for an Italian Catholic girl to marry an Italian Jewish Episcopalian.

FIORELLO (*Dry*) You chose the right person to ask all right.

THEA You know what he said?

FIORELLO Of course, I know. What could he say? But I notice something else.

THEA What?

FIORELLO I notice you're thinking about marrying me or you wouldn't have asked him.

THEA   Oh—you noticed that.

FIORELLO   Yes, and I notice something else.

THEA   What else?

FIORELLO   I know you're not going out steady with any of these lounge lizards who are hanging around you.

THEA   Oh!

FIORELLO   So quit arguing. After I get Trieste for you—when I come back—

THEA   (*Impulsive*)   Not for me—for justice! That's why we should get Trieste!

FIORELLO   I'm going to capture it for you, personally.

THEA   Oh, Fiorello, if you do—
   (*She kisses him on the cheek*)

FIORELLO   If I do, you're going to have to kiss me better than that. (*Starts to embrace her, but there is a knock at the door*) Who is it?
   (MORRIS *sticks his head in*)

MORRIS   I think we'd better get this done before they close in on you, Mr. LaGuardia.

FIORELLO   Oh, yes, of course, come in, Morris. (MORRIS *and* MARIE *enter*) Marie, give me those papers. I'll sign them. Let's get it over with.
   (*He sits at the table and signs papers as* MARIE *places them in front of him one at a time*)

THEA   Morris, you think your wife will let you dance with me?

MORRIS (*Giving her his arm*) She better, after all the money I spent at Roseland!

    (*They go out into the yard*)

FIORELLO There—and those—I hope you checked them.

MARIE Yes, I did.

FIORELLO (*Touches her hand as she gathers the papers*) Thank you, Marie, for many things. (*He looks out the window*) Now, look at that—isn't that pretty? I like dancing.

MARIE I do, too.

FIORELLO You do? That's a surprise to me. All right, come on now, let's see if we can keep in step.

    (*They dance awkwardly in the room, while the set revolves and opens up, revealing the yard. Everyone is dancing. Many men are in uniform. All the girls wear party frocks. BEN mounts a platform. The crowd grows quiet and waits*)

BEN And now, friends, it's time to say good-bye. My boy (*Puts a hand on FIORELLO's shoulder*)—in addition to all the other great things he's done down there in Washington—he's now going over there to clean up the map of Europe for good old Uncle Sam. (*Applause*) Ladies and gentlemen, with all our thanks and all our best wishes, and a prayer from right here in our hearts—we say good-bye and good luck and God bless you and give the Kaiser a good swift kick you-know-where from all of us. (*Crowd laughs*) Captain LaGuardia has asked for no speechmaking. Instead he thinks we'd all like music.

    (*He motions to THEA to lead singing*)

THEA (*Sings "Till Tomorrow"*)
    Twilight descends

Everything ends
Till tomorrow, tomorrow

Since we must part
Here is my heart
Till tomorrow, tomorrow

Clouds drifting by
Echo a sigh
Parting is such sweet sorrow

I'm drifting, too, .
Dreaming of you
Till tomorrow comes.

COMPANY (*Final chorus*)
Twilight descends
Everything ends
Till tomorrow, tomorrow

Since we must part
Here is my heart
Till tomorrow, tomorrow

Clouds drifting by
Echo a sigh
Parting is such sweet sorrow

I'm drifting, too,
Dreaming of you
Till tomorrow comes.

Blackout

A movie screen is lowered.

> *Picture:* The Pathé News roos-
> ter crowing.

Caption: CAMP DIX, NEW JERSEY
First Draftees Report for Training

> *Picture:* American draftees in
> camp having their
> teeth examined.

Caption: WASHINGTON, D.C.
Flying Congressman, F. H. LaGuardia, Clears Desk
on Which He Helped Shape the Draft Act.

> *Picture:* Fiorello in civilian
> clothes at his desk,
> busily signing papers.

Caption: SOMEWHERE IN FRANCE
LaGuardia Squadron Prepares for Action

> *Picture:* Fiorello and his men
> gathered around a bi-
> plane.

Caption: ACTION!

> *Picture:* Aerial dogfight.

Caption: The Major's First Scalp!

> *Picture:* Fiorello in close-up at controls of plane. German plane is hit, plummets to earth.

Caption: TRIESTE
King Victor Emmanuel Reclaims Trieste for Italy

> *Picture:* Victor Emmanuel amid cheering throng.

Caption: Trieste's Favorite Son

> *Picture:* Fiorello in flier's uniform.

Caption: "Aw, shucks, it was nothing."

> *Picture:* Fiorello rocking back and forth and smiling shyly at camera.

Caption: ARMISTICE

> *Picture:* Exultant throngs, Times Square, newspapers proclaiming Armistice, flags waving, etc.

Caption: NEW YORK HARBOR:
HOME AGAIN!
(*The orchestra underscores "Home Again"*)

> *Picture:* Troop ship entering New York Harbor, passing the Statue of Liberty, pulling into a

> dock, soldiers waving
> and coming down
> gangplank.

(The picture dissolves into a real gangplank. The stage is full of returning soldiers. FIORELLO walks to the gangplank. The crowd cheers)

FIORELLO   My friends—it's good to be back in this wonderful country—this wonderful city. It's good to be home.

COMPANY *(Singing softly, "Home Again")*
Home again
Home again
What a day

Home again
Home again
Home again to stay.
(FIORELLO walks down the gangplank, passes the eagerly waiting MARIE, hurries to THEA)

FIORELLO   Thea, I brought you a present—a key to the city— Trieste.

THEA   Oh, Fiorello!

FIORELLO   Now what's the score?

THEA   Yes!
(They embrace. The crowd sings "Home Again" while confetti falls)

COMPANY
Home again
Home again

Home to stay

Home again
Home again
In the U.S.A.

Curtain

ACT TWO

Scene One

Place: The LAGUARDIA *home.*

At rise: THEA, *wearing a kimono and mules, is setting out breakfast. From the bedroom, offstage,* FIORELLO's *voice is heard raised cheerily in a snatch of opera. The phone rings.* THEA *hurries to answer it.*

THEA *(Into phone)* Hello? Yes, this is Mrs. LaGuardia. Put him on. Oh, hello, Ben—
    (FIORELLO *stops singing*)

FIORELLO *(Enters from the bedroom. He wears a shirt, tie, underdrawers. No pants)* Hey, honeybunch! I can't find my pants.

THEA Ben wants to talk to you.

FIORELLO Where's my black suit? *(Sits down beside her and takes the phone)* Yes, Ben? I said what? My war record? What's the matter with it? I don't care if it was ten years ago—facts are facts. I'm busy, Ben. Good-bye. *(To* THEA*)* Thinks I talked too much about my war record in that interview. These nickel-and-dime ward heelers! Where's my black suit?

THEA In the kitchen. I'm sending it out to be pressed.

FIORELLO *(Crosses toward the kitchen door)* How do you expect me to beat Jimmy Walker if I wear pressed pants?
    (The phone rings. He exits into the kitchen)

THEA (*Into phone*) Hello. Oh, Ben—I'm sorry. You know how he is on the first day of the campaign. (*She stops as* FIORELLO *re-enters. He is carrying a crumpled black suit all balled up in a wad under his arm*) Oh, darling, no, you're not going to wear that!

FIORELLO (*Surprised, as he shakes out the crumpled suit*) Why not?

THEA You're an important man. You're running for Mayor. You can't go around looking like a—

FIORELLO I've got a big speech at a Hundred Twenty-fifth Street tonight. I want to look like the people I'll be talking to. Not like that tinhorn tailor's dummy they've got down in City Hall.
(*He exits into the bedroom*)

THEA (*Into phone*) Ben, he's busy just now. Can I take a message. All right, I understand. (*The door buzzer sounds*) Good-bye.
(THEA *hangs up and hurries to answer the door*)

FIORELLO'S VOICE (*Shouts*) Hey, honeybunch! Those notes I was making last night on my speech?

DORA (*Offstage*) Hello!

THEA Hello!
(DORA *enters wearing street clothes*)

DORA I hope you don't mind my dropping in on you like this, Thea.

THEA Of course not, Dora.

DORA Floyd's got another job.

THEA Another one?

DORA Every year another promotion. I'm so excited.

FIORELLO (*Enters, wearing pants and fastening his belt*) Hi, Dora.

DORA Good morning, Mr. LaGuardia.

THEA They're right here, darling!

FIORELLO (*Taking the papers from* THEA) How's the sewer business?

DORA That's what I came over to tell Thea about. I'm so excited. Floyd's just given up sewers.

FIORELLO Too bad. I thought it suited him.
(*He disappears into the bedroom with the papers*)

THEA You mustn't mind Fiorello's jokes about Floyd.
(*They go to the table, where* THEA *pours coffee*)

DORA Oh, I don't mind. You ought to hear what Floyd says about him. Politics! Ish-ke-bibble—we just have to go along with our men—that's all. Guess what happened? Floyd's going into garbage!

THEA Is that better than sewers?

DORA He has the city's disposal contract for lower Manhattan.
(FIORELLO *comes in. He is buttoning his vest with one hand*)

FIORELLO There was a yellow sheet, with some figures, the amount of city funds Walker spent to put a private steam room into his City Hall office.

THEA Right here, darling.

FIORELLO Oh—thanks.
(*He exits*)

THEA Well, I'm very happy for you and Floyd.

DORA Thea, it's just wonderful. The people we meet and the social events. The other night at Luchow's Jimmy Hines stopped and said, "How do you do," and Al Smith was practically next to me—except on the other side of the restaurant. Honestly! I'm so excited!
(*The phone rings*)

THEA (*Into phone*) Hello? Oh, hello, Ben. No, I haven't had a chance yet. He's—(FIORELLO *appears at the bedroom door, studying notes*) Wait a minute, Ben. (*To* FIORELLO, *as she puts down the phone*) He's calling back about your speech tonight. (FIORELLO *is crossing toward the phone*) Ben thinks you should let somebody else represent you uptown, while you go out to Staten Island tonight and—

FIORELLO (*Stops moving toward the phone and, annoyed, turns*) Tell him to stick to poker and I'll stick to running my own campaign!
(*He exits into the bedroom*)

DORA Well, I've got to run. I'm meeting Floyd at our new penthouse. That's what he got me to celebrate the promotion.

THEA (*Walking* DORA *to the door, she picks up the phone*) He's sweet as well as loyal. Give him my best.

DORA I will, darling.
(*She exits*)

THEA Good-bye, Dora. (*Into phone*) I'm sorry, Ben. I can't get him now. But I'll give him your message.

DORA (*Re-enters*) Oh, gosh, isn't this awful?

THEA Yes, Ben. Good-bye.
(*She hangs up*)

DORA I'm so excited about Floyd, I forgot all about you! Thea, what did the doctor say?

THEA (*Glancing nervously toward the bedroom door*) It's nothing, nothing at all.

DORA You sure?

THEA Forget it, please. Forget I ever said a word. I'm all right. I'm a little tired, the doctor says, and maybe a little run-down, and all I need is rest.

DORA Well, now, you see that you get it. You hear?

THEA Of course I will.

DORA Because health, boy, I'm telling you, Thea, without your health you can have swell clothes, and be going out in society and everything wonderful, and you have one little pain in your stomach and the whole thing gives you a pain in the stomach. You know what I mean? Take care of yourself.

(*She exits.* FIORELLO *enters, now completely dressed, and goes toward the breakfast table*)

FIORELLO   Well, I'm on my way. (*Suddenly stops and looks through his pockets*) Wait a minute—I had some figures on Alderman Marconi's bank deposits. (*Finds the papers*) Oh, here they are.
          (*He sits down and sips coffee hastily as he fusses with the papers*)

THEA   Joe Marconi?

FIORELLO (*Grimly*)   The same.

THEA   Is he in trouble?

FIORELLO   Now, honeybunch, I know he heads the charity for Trieste and all the Italians are soft on him, but a crook is a crook. If Morris or Marie call, tell them I'm on my way.

THEA   I haven't seen Marie in weeks. Why don't you ask her to dinner some night?

FIORELLO   All right, honeybunch, when you're feeling a little stronger.

THEA   Is she going steady with anyone now?

FIORELLO   How do I know? You women!

THEA   Well, she should get married.

FIORELLO   Then what'll I do?

THEA   Darling!
          (THEA *gives him a reproving glance*)

FIORELLO   No, I didn't mean it. If she finds the right man, I'll scream to high heaven, but I'll be happy for her. (*He rises, kisses her, and goes to door as he talks. She follows*) Now don't send any more suits out to be pressed until this campaign is over. I don't know when I'll be home. This rally starts at eleven. But if you're still awake, and you keep your window open, around about midnight you should hear a long loud scream. (*He gives* THEA *another quick kiss and snatches up his ten-gallon hat*) That will be Jimmy Walker yelling Uncle!

(*He slaps the hat on his head and exits.* THEA *stares after him for a moment. Standing alone, she sings the ballad: "When Did I Fall in Love?"*)

THEA (*Singing*)

There he goes, my Congressman,
Starting his day hurrying right to a fight
There he goes, Sir Galahad,
Galloping off, riding his white Willy's-Knight.

Out of the house ten seconds and I miss him
I miss him more with each good-bye
Out of the house ten seconds and I miss him
And no one's more astonished than I.
I never once pretended that I loved him
When did it start
This change of heart?

When did I fall in love
What night
Which day
When did I first begin to feel this way

How could the moment pass
Unfelt

Ignored
Where was the blinding flash
Where was the crashing chord

When did I fall in love
I can't recall
Not that it matters at all
It doesn't matter when, or why, or how
As long as I love him now.
When did respect first become affection
When did affection suddenly soar
What a strange and beautiful touch
That I love him so much
When I didn't before.

When did I fall in love
What night
Which day
When did I first begin to feel this way
How could the moment pass
Unfelt
Ignored
Where was the blinding flash
Where was the crashing chord

When did I fall in love
I can't recall
Not that it matters at all
I'm where I want to be
His love, his wife
Until the end of my life.

Blackout

Eileen Rodgers as MITZI

Scene Two

Place: The terrace of FLOYD *and* DORA MCDUFF's *penthouse home.*

At rise: The butler is putting a punch bowl down on the table. DORA *enters.*

DORA Chadwick!

BUTLER Yes, madame?

DORA Did you fix a place for the actresses to change?

BUTLER Yes, madame, in the blue room.

DORA Oh, good.
  (FLOYD *enters*)

FLOYD Say, Chadwick, the bootlegger's late, so we better get out some of that gin I made last week.

BUTLER Very good, sir.
  (*The* BUTLER *goes out*)

FLOYD (*Disappointed*) Jimmy Hines ain't coming. He just phoned, but a lot of other big Tammany politicians will be here so I want everything to go off swell.

DORA I don't see how it can be so swell when they aren't even bringing their wives.

FLOYD   It's a business meeting.

DORA   With a lot of chorus girls?

FLOYD   With a celebrated music comedy star—Mitzi Travers.

DORA   Oh sure, and those others down there—you ought to hear them. "It's cute!—You're cute!—I'm cute!"

FLOYD   Listen, stupid—Jimmy Hines is givin' me the honor of running this rally. You ought to be proud I asked those big shots here.

DORA   Big shots! And a gangster like Frankie Scarpini—what's he doing here?

FLOYD   The Commissioner wants to see him. Now mind your own business or I'll give you a clout.
(*He raises his hand to strike her. She faces up to him, nose to nose*)

DORA (*Chin out*)   Just you try it! Just you try it! Just once!
(FLOYD *falters, drops his hand, crosses, and sits*)

FLOYD (*Defeated, pleading*)   Listen, Dora. I asked him here because I wanted to show off the penthouse, and the oil paintings and everything. Dora, please, I don't care about those girls. I ain't never looked at no other dame but you since we first met up.

DORA (*Contrite*)   I'm sorry. (*She sits in his lap*) I'll be good.
(*Voices are heard offstage.* DORA *gets off* FLOYD's *lap. The* JUDGE *enters*)

JUDGE   Evening, Floyd.

98

FLOYD   Oh, Judge, come on in. Sweetheart, you know Judge Carter.

DORA   How do you do, Judge?
(DORA *goes out*)

JUDGE   Nice place you got here, Floyd.

FLOYD   It's comfortable. It's home. By the way, Judge, the Chief wanted me to thank you for your help in killing that indictment. Nice to know we can count on you.

JUDGE   Thank you.
(*Several men enter*)

COMMISSIONER   Well, I'm telling you—

POLITICIAN   Nobody pays any attention to what LaGuardia says.

COMMISSIONER   I'm getting damn sick and tired of being insulted by that man. And so is Hines and Marconi and a lot of others.

POLITICIAN   But if the public thinks we get a hoodlum like Frank Scarpini to—?

COMMISSIONER   The public won't think—'cause they won't know.

FLOYD   Commissioner—everybody knows that LaGuardia is just a loudmouth.

COMMISSIONER   Suppose he was saying these things about you?

POLITICIAN   Maybe we could shut Fiorello up if we could get something on him.

99

FLOYD What?

A MAN How about women?

FLOYD Women, hell—he won't even listen to a dirty story. Not a chance.

JUDGE Floyd, how about letting him get hit by a truck?

FLOYD I don't know if it's practical. He's awful fast on his feet. (*Enter several chorus girls*)

CUTIE All right for we girls to come out here?

FLOYD Come right along, certainly.

CUTIE Oh, this is cute. Oh, what a gorgeous view. You can see the roof of our theatre.
(DORA *enters, followed by* MITZI)

DORA Floyd, here's Miss Travers.

MITZI How nice!

FLOYD Gentlemen—the star of the evening. Miss Mitzi Travers.

FIRST MAN Miss Travers.

FOURTH MAN Nice to have you on our side, Miss Travers.

MITZI I don't know much about politics, although I certainly hope I'm not stupid.

FLOYD All right, folks, now let's pay attention. Maybe we'll put this song just in front of Jimmy Walker's big speech. Intro-

ducing that wonderful little actress, the golden-voiced star of
Yoo-Hoo Yah-Hoo, Miss Mitzi Travers!
> (FLOYD *applauds*)

MITZI (*Sings "Gentleman Jimmy"*)
> Live and let live
> Love and let love
> There are no finer sentiments than those
>
> Live and let live
> Love and let love
> That's what Jimmy tells the world
> Where e'er he goes
>
> In London, in Paris
> Bermuda and Rome
> They love him
> Just like we do at home
>
> Who's that genial gentleman in the
> Silk hat
> Gray spats
> Striped pants
> Why that's
> Gotta be him
> Gentleman Jimmy
>
> Who's that swell celebrity with the
> Glad hand
> Quick wit
> New York's
> Fav'rite
> That'll be him
> Gentleman Jimmy

Say, Jim, we promise on voting day
We will love you in November as we do in May
Hey!

Who's that dapper happy-go-lucky
Son of Broadway
We love James J. Walker.

Why, he's as graceful as Fred Astaire
He's the man who kept the subway to a five-cent fare
So there!

Who's that dapper, happy-go-lucky
Son of Broadway
We love James J.
'Cause under him Manhattan is just a
Syn . . . o . . . nym for
Generous . . . Gentleman . . .
James J. Walker!
    (*The girls all talk at the end of the song*)

FIRST CUTIE   You were wonderful!

SECOND CUTIE   That'll be the biggest hit!

THIRD CUTIE   It's cute! It's so cute!

FOURTH CUTIE   And so meaning! The words and everything!

FLOYD   Well, we all agree that goes in.

ANOTHER MAN   That'll be the hit of the rally, Miss Travers.
    (*Enter* FRANK SCARPINI *with* BODYGUARDS) Hi, Frankie!

FIRST MAN   Oh—here's Frankie.

FRANKIE (*To* BODYGUARDS)   Okay, boys.
(BODYGUARDS *exit*)

COMMISSIONER   Come on in. We've been waiting for you.

FLOYD   All right, girls. Now let's see what you're going to do.

CUTIE   Where's our shoes? I gave that man our shoes. (*Enter* BUTLER) Oh—here they are.

DORA   This way, girls.
(*She leads the girls out to the blue room*)

COMMISSIONER (*To* SCARPINI)   We've been talking over that little problem.

MITZI (*To* FLOYD)   I could introduce my number by saying that I'm a personal friend of Jimmy's.

FLOYD   I tell you, Mitzi, Mr. Hines says let's keep personal things out of it—on account of possible trouble with—you know.

FRANKIE (*To* COMMISSIONER)   When he makes this speech at a Hundred Sixth Street—

COMMISSIONER   That's next week!

FRANKIE   Yah—(DORA *enters and crosses to* FLOYD. FRANKIE *leans close to the* COMMISSIONER) Well, here's the idea.

DORA (*To* FLOYD *as she eyes* SCARPINI)   I think he's a terrible-looking man.

FLOYD (*Nervous*)   Easy, kid, he'll hear you. He ain't so bad when you get to know him.

DORA   Is there one good thing about him?

FLOYD   Yes. He's loyal.

DORA   He's very mean-looking.

FLOYD   For God's sake, keep quiet. You want to get me bumped off?

COMMISSIONER   There's a roof right over the platform where he's going to speak.

FRANKIE   The Commish—he's not so dumb.

COMMISSIONER   And you'll have somebody up there ready to drop it on him, is that it?

FRANKIE   We'll brain him—don't worry.

POLITICIAN   But what's this about the fire alarm?
     (CUTIE *enters*)

CUTIE   You ready for we girls?

FLOYD   All ready, gentlemen?

COMMISSIONER   Maybe Frankie and I should go downstairs and—?

FRANKIE (*Ogling the* CUTIES)   No, wait. I want to see the to-matoes.

FLOYD   Okay, kids.

CUTIE   Line up, everybody.

FLOYD   If we like this, we can tack it right on to Mitzi's song.

CUTIE   Oh, Mr. McDuff, you'll like it. It's very original.
(*The girls come out, tap dancing to the "Gentleman Jimmy" music*)

GIRLS' FEET
Clomp, Clomp, Clomp
Clippety Cloppety . . .

CUTIE
Hey-hey!

GIRLS' FEET
Tap tap tap . . .

Blackout

SCENE THREE

Place: FIORELLO'S *law office.*

At rise: In the private office, FIORELLO *is seated behind his desk. A* REPORTER *is in the chair beside the desk.* BEN MARINO *is standing at one side. In the outer office,* MARIE *is at the filing cabinet.* NEIL, *now more mature-looking than when we last saw him, is working at a desk.* MORRIS, *who also looks older, is talking on the phone. A new girl,* FLORENCE, *is at the switchboard.*

MORRIS (*Patient, dead-pan, into phone*) Shirley, I just don't know. Listen, dear—election will be over in another week. Then I'll get some friends to introduce us. And I'll come to dinner nearly every night.
(*Enter* MR. ZAPPATELLA)

MR. ZAPPATELLA (*To* FLORENCE) I come see Mr. LaGuardia, please?

NEIL (*Calls*) Oh, hello, Mr. Zappatella.

MR. ZAPPATELLA (*Turning from* FLORENCE *to* NEIL) Counselor, do I got the house?

NEIL You certainly have. Here, sit down, please. (*He motions to the chair beside his desk.* MR. ZAPPATELLA *takes it*) Mr. La Guardia couldn't attend the closing himself, so I appeared as the attorney of record. If you'll just sign here, please.
(*He places some papers in front of* MR. ZAPPATELLA *and*

hands him a pen. MR. ZAPPATELLA *begins very laboriously to sign his name*)

MORRIS (*Into phone*) Shirley, you and the twins go ahead and eat. Me, I'll just—

NEIL (*Indicating another place on the documents*) And here, please.
(MR. ZAPPATELLA *begins again the laborious business of signing his name*)

MORRIS (*Irritable, into phone*) I can't help it if they're forgetting what their daddy looks like. Sometimes I can't remember myself. (*He hangs up and addresses* MARIE) Be happy you're not married.

MARIE Oh yeah?

MORRIS (*Contrite*) Marie!

MARIE (*Pinches his cheek forgivingly*) You're cute.
(*The voices die down in the outer office and come up in the inner office*)

REPORTER (*Wad of folded copy paper and pencil in hand*) Would you mind repeating that, Mr. LaGuardia?

FIORELLO I said, when the ballot boxes are opened you will find that I have beaten Mayor Walker by at least three hundred and fifty thousand votes.

REPORTER (*Scribbling*) Three hundred and fifty thousand.

FIORELLO If the weather is good, you can raise that figure to half a million. The voters know me, they know my war record.
(BEN MARINO *rolls his eyes to heaven in disgust*)

REPORTER Then you expect to keep the Italian vote?

FIORELLO (*Rising*) Now, look here, young man—what do you
mean by that?

BEN (*Warningly*) Major!

FIORELLO Why shouldn't I keep the Italian vote?

REPORTER I thought maybe—

FIORELLO You thought what? Come on, don't waste my time
with a lot of mumbling. What did you think maybe?

REPORTER You called Alderman Marconi a crook.

FIORELLO Well, isn't he?

REPORTER He's very popular with the Italian people.

FIORELLO I didn't call him a crook. I called him a thief. A chisel-
ing tinhorn pickpocket who has robbed the city for years.

REPORTER May I print that?

FIORELLO In capital letters.

REPORTER Thank you, Mr. LaGuardia.
(*He goes*)

FIORELLO I guess that will hold him.

BEN (*Slowly*) I guess so.
(*He starts for the door*)

FIORELLO Where you going?

BEN   For some fresh air. (*Pauses, looks at* FIORELLO, *then starts out again*) See you tonight.

FIORELLO   Ben! (BEN *stops*) What's the matter with you?

BEN   I've got a delicate stomach. Some kinds of things upset me.

FIORELLO   Like what?

BEN   Like the way you been running this campaign, Major.

FIORELLO   You think you can do better?

BEN   I could make a few suggestions.

FIORELLO   Like the way you did in that lousy district of yours before I took it over?

BEN   I thought you'd bring that up.

FIORELLO   Just to remind you that I've been right, and you've been wrong. That's all.

BEN   Yes, Major, you've been right, and you've done a hell of a lot of things that nobody thought you could, but once in a while you used to listen to some of us dumb bastards make a suggestion. You're going to lose, Major. Why? Because you can't play ball—not for one minute. We all know about your war record. We all know how incorruptible you are. You don't have to prove it so many times a day. You had to throw the Italian vote out the window to prove you're a fearless leader. You're not trying to win an election. You're just hoping that someday they'll put your statue up in Central Park.

FIORELLO   That's quite a speech, Ben.

BEN   That's the short version.

FIORELLO   Well, take it home and work on it—and don't come back.

BEN   I'll come back.

FIORELLO (*Furious*)   I don't need you. I don't want you. Get out of here. (*The phone rings*) Good-bye.

BEN   Good-bye, Major. (BEN *goes to outer office and, as he exits, he addresses* FIORELLO's *staff*) So long, chumps.
(*The phone rings.* FIORELLO *grabs it*)

FIORELLO (*Angry, into phone*)   I told you I don't want to be bothered!

FLORENCE   Mr. LaGuardia, it's Doctor Marsini. He says—

FIORELLO   Oh. Oh, well—yes—I'll talk to him.
(DORA *enters the outer office from the street*)

DORA   Marie!

MARIE   Dora, come on in.

FLORENCE (*Into phone*)   All right, Dr. Marsini, here's Mr. La Guardia.

FIORELLO (*Into his phone*)   That's all right. Of course, of course.

DORA   I gotta talk to you, Marie. Very private.

MARIE   My gosh. Something wrong? Sure, dear, right over here.
(*She leads* DORA *to a deserted corner of the outer office*)

NEIL (*Jogging the documents into a neat pile*)   That does it, Mr. Zappatella, the house is yours.
> (FIORELLO *has finished talking on the phone. He hangs up and comes into the outer office*)

FIORELLO   Florence, get my wife, please.

MR. ZAPPATELLA   Thank you, Mr. LaGuardia. I now can tell my Rosa it's true. We got our own house.
> (*He exits*)

FLORENCE   I have Mrs. LaGuardia.
> (FIORELLO *hurries back into his private office and picks up the phone*)

DORA (*To* MARIE)   Now remember, you promised. And you've got to make him promise.

MARIE   Oh, he will, Dora. You don't have to worry about that. I know Mr. LaGuardia will feel the way I do, that you've been a real friend.

DORA   Gee whiz, Marie, a person gets so mixed up. I want to be loyal to Floyd. He's really a good, decent person, really he is. But I also can't forget what Mr. LaGuardia once did for all of us. Gee, I want to do the right thing.

MARIE   You did. You don't have to worry about it, Dora. Nobody will ever know. I promised. I double promised.
> (DORA *nods her head, believing* MARIE, *and goes out.* MARIE *sees her as far as the door*)

FIORELLO (*On the phone in the inner office*)   Now, honeybunch, what's the use of paying the doctor good money if you don't do what he tells you to do? You've heard me make speeches before, and you'll hear me make plenty more. So you can forget about this one tonight and take care of yourself. I want you to go to bed and stay there. The doctor says you need rest. (MARIE *knocks on his office door*. FIORELLO *turns toward the door*) Well—? (MARIE *sticks her head in*. FIORELLO *speaks into phone*) I've got to hang up now, Thea. (*To* MARIE) Come in, Marie. (MARIE *enters. He continues into phone*) Something important has come up. Now I want you to listen, honeybunch. You go to bed. And when I come home, I'll do the whole damn speech over for you. Is that clear? You bet. You bet your life. Now, you do that. Good-bye. (*Hangs up. To* MARIE) What's wrong?

MARIE   First, Mr. LaGuardia, you must understand—what I'm going to tell you is an absolute secret.

FIORELLO   I understand.

MARIE   Absolute!

FIORELLO   Marie, I said I understand.

MARIE   Because Dora could get in terrible trouble.

FIORELLO   Nobody's getting into trouble. Now spill it.

MARIE   Dora heard some men talking to her husband. They're going to start some trouble at your speech tonight.

FIORELLO   Oh, they are?

MARIE   First they're going to turn in a fire alarm at Madison and a Hundred and Fifth. Then some other thugs are going to be up on a roof and they're going to have a baby carriage full of paving blocks. And then in all the excitement they're going to push it off the roof on top of your head!

FIORELLO Now, isn't that typical? Good! It shows they're frightened.

MARIE But it's murder! They're going to try to kill you!

FIORELLO (*Striding to the outer office*) The whole damn German air force tried that once, and look what happened to them! (*At the door*) Neil!

NEIL Yes, Major?

FIORELLO Morris!

MORRIS (*Who has been talking on the phone*) Never mind, Shirley, give the twins my share.
(*He hangs up and, with* NEIL, *hurries after* FIORELLO *into the private office*)

FIORELLO (*After they have shut the door*) Neil.

NEIL Yes, Major?

FIORELLO There's a fire-alarm box at Madison and a Hundred and Fifth. During my speech tonight, someone may try to send in an alarm. Don't let him. Got it?

NEIL Yes, sir. (*Pause*) Suppose there's a fire?

FIORELLO Not tonight! Your job is to see that nobody pulls that lever. Morris, get hold of someone at headquarters and have some guards put on the roof over the platform where I'm speaking. If they see any baby carriages, throw them down the stairs.

MORRIS (*Stunned*)   Major! Baby carriages?

FIORELLO   They'll be full of paving blocks. Well, Neil, what about it? Get moving.

NEIL   I was just thinking, Major, suppose it's a policeman?

FIORELLO   Tell him if the law won't protect us, we'll have to protect ourselves. Get tough with him. And if you have to—hit him. Don't hesitate.

NEIL (*Incredulous*)   Sock a cop?

FIORELLO   Yes. Punch him in the eye. Come on, get moving.
(*He leads the way out, followed by* MORRIS *and* NEIL)

MORRIS (*To* FLORENCE)   Call Shirley and tell her I'm in jail.

Blackout

Scene Four

Place: Madison Avenue and One Hundred and Fifth Street. There is a fire-alarm box downstage left.

At rise: We can hear sounds of a political rally: FIORELLO'S *voice rising and falling, occasional cheers, etc.* NEIL *walks up and down, looking around, on guard. Three young men walk through from left to right.*

FIRST MAN   It's a rally. You know, speeches, vote for me, I'm a great guy.

SECOND MAN   Jimmy Walker?

FIRST MAN   No, no, it's that nut LaGuardia. What a kill-joy that guy is. He wants to reform everything. Geez, I think Jimmy Walker's got the right idea.
  (*They go out.* NEIL *has strolled over right. A* TOUGH MAN *comes in furtively and goes over to the alarm box. He un-hooks the little hammer to break the glass.* NEIL *hurries up to him*)

NEIL   Hey! What are you doing?

TOUGH MAN   Just reading this here sign. Got any objections?

NEIL   Got no objection to your reading.

TOUGH MAN   All right, mister, then how's about minding your own business?

NEIL   Just don't pull the handle.

TOUGH MAN   Why not shouldn't I pull the handle?

NEIL   'Cause the fire department is tired.

TOUGH MAN   And what's that to you?

NEIL (*Sore*)   I'm on duty here. I got orders not to bother the fire department tonight, see?

TOUGH MAN (*Giving* NEIL *a wide berth*)   Good for you. (*Turns and retreats*) I got a couple of friends I'll tell about that.
   (*He goes off. Cheers are heard offstage. Two men and a woman walk through from left to right*)

DERBY   What do you mean vote Republican? They're against the people, ain't they?

FEDORA   Vote Independent, I say.

DERBY   That's a lot of malarkey. What does that get you?
   (*As they go out, a* FRANTIC MAN *runs in left and seizes the little metal hammer of the fire-alarm box*)

FRANTIC   Fire! Fire!

NEIL (*Grabs him and shoves him away*)   Just a second, buddy. Keep your hands off that!

FRANTIC   There's a fire!

NEIL   Keep your hands off that!

FRANTIC   My room is on fire! (NEIL *pushes him back again*) The building is burning up!

116

NEIL   Let it burn.

FRANTIC   Get out of my way, I tell you! (NEIL *pushes him back violently and he falls*) God damn you, you'll pay for this. Are you crazy? What's the matter with you?
  (*He gets up*)

NEIL   I don't think there is any fire.

FRANTIC   My house is on fire, I tell you!

NEIL   Where do you live?

FRANTIC   Huh?

NEIL   I thought so. Well, you can just wait until after the speech is over to have your house burn down.

FRANTIC   Wise guy, huh?
  (*A couple of other tough-looking characters enter to back up* FRANTIC. MORRIS *enters*)

MORRIS   Neil.

NEIL   Just in time, Morris. I may want you to identify this guy in court.

FRANTIC   I'll show you some identifying, you fresh mug. Me and one or two others.
  (*He joins his gang, and they go out to reconnoiter. Cheers are heard offstage*)

NEIL   (*To* MORRIS)   This is a busy little assignment the Major gave me. How long do you suppose before he's finished with that speech?

MORRIS   Neil—I got a message.

NEIL   Message?

MORRIS   Neil—she died—Mrs. LaGuardia. They called up—I didn't know what to do.

NEIL   But it can't be!

MORRIS   About an hour ago.

NEIL   God damn!

MORRIS   Come on, Neil, I got a car out there.

NEIL   Sure, sure.
(*They hurry out. Cheers offstage.* FRANTIC, *backed up by several others, comes in. He looks around, see there is no guard, and rushes to the alarm box. He breaks the glass and pulls the lever and they quickly disappear in all directions. The speech is heard offstage for a second; there are cheers. Then the sounds of the fire-alarm sirens become audible and gradually grow until they fill the theatre*)

Blackout

Place: FIORELLO'S *office.*

At rise: MARIE *is alone. She wears a hat. She stands at the switchboard, talking into phone.*

MARIE (*Distressed*)   And then the problem of his speeches. He has about twenty speeches scheduled between now and election. No, Doctor. We haven't been able to reach him yet. He's still on the speaker's platform. But Morris and Neil are there. As soon as he finishes speaking, they'll—(*Enter* MORRIS *and* NEIL) Here they are now. Good-bye, Doctor. (*She hangs up*) Did you tell him?

MORRIS   No.

MARIE   No?

MORRIS   We couldn't get to him.

NEIL   That baby carriage full of paving blocks. They dropped it—

MORRIS   I could kill myself.

NEIL   And in all the excitement—

MARIE   Is he hurt?
        (*Enter* FIORELLO, *his face smudged, his clothes dirty, his manner sardonic*)

FIORELLO   How the hell would they know?

MARIE (*Frightened by his appearance*)   Mr. LaGuardia, you're hurt!

FIORELLO (*Impatient*)   No, no. All I need is a whisk broom and some soap and water. I can't go home looking like this. Get Thea on the phone. She'd have a relapse if she saw me like this. Thanks to them. (*Jerks his head sarcastically toward* MORRIS *and* NEIL *as he slaps dust from his jacket*) What a team! You got any bridges that have to be held? Send for these two! They'll foul things up but good. Any of your dikes spring a leak lately? Send for Neil and Morris, and watch your whole damn country get flooded away before the night's over! (*To* NEIL) Where were you when that alarm was pulled? (*To* MORRIS) Did you have anybody on that roof? Or were you just too damn busy on the phone telling Shirley when to put the roast in?

MORRIS (*Halting*)   Something happened—

FIORELLO   You bet it did. Or almost, anyway. Next time I want protection, I know two guys I'll send in the opposite direction.

MORRIS   Major, Dr. Marsini called.

FIORELLO   The doctor?

MARIE   Yes.

FIORELLO   Dr. Marsini?

MORRIS   I pulled Neil away from the fire-alarm box because—

FIORELLO (*Sharp*)   Is Thea worse?

MARIE   It was my fault.
   (*They stare helplessly at him*)

FIORELLO   Well, come on, what is it? (*To* MARIE) What are you doing here at night?

MARIE   Morris called me.

MORRIS   It happened very suddenly. Dr. Marsini tried to—he—Major, it happened—that's why—it happened—the worst—she died.
   (FIORELLO *reacts, then turns quickly and goes out*)

NEIL   Should we go with him?

MORRIS   No, no, leave him alone.

NEIL   Sure.
   (*He bolts out door*)

MORRIS   Marie, will you close the office?

MARIE   I will. Yes.
   (MORRIS *goes. She turns out lights in inner office, then stands motionless and looks straight forward*)

Blackout

SCENE SIX

Out of the darkness comes the voice of a radio ANNOUNCER.

ANNOUNCER'S VOICE . . . several more hours, of course, before
the final tabulations are complete. But it is perfectly clear now
that James J. Walker has been returned to office by one of the
most overwhelming landslides ever rolled up by a candidate
in this city. Out of a total of just slightly less than one million,
two hundred thousand votes cast, Fiorello LaGuardia has gone
down to defeat by well over half a million ballots.
> (*During the radio speech the sound of crowds cheering
> becomes louder and louder, and when the lights come on,
> the stage is filled with jubilant celebrants who sing and
> dance their victory song,* "*Gentleman Jimmy*")

COMPANY
We kept our promise on voting day
That we'd love you in November
As we did in May
Hey!

Who's that dapper happy-go-lucky
Son of Broadway
We love James J.
'Cause under him Manhattan is just a
Synonym for generous Gentleman James
That's him
That's Jimmy . . . Jimmy . . . Jimmy

Jimmy . . . Jimmy . . . Jimmy . . . Jimmy
> (*Dancers and singers exit.* FIORELLO, MARIE, MORRIS, NEIL
> *come in. They move slowly, a defeated group*)

NEIL (*A sudden eruption*)   Major, it's just rotten luck.

FIORELLO (*Stops and turns*)   Luck! Luck has nothing to do with
it. Don't you know the people always vote for the better man?

MARIE (*Angry*)   You know that isn't so. He's not fit to shine
your shoes. You know that.

FIORELLO   Damn right I do! (*Pause*) I beg your pardon, Marie.

MARIE   Oh, I've heard the word before. I've said it quite a few
times tonight, too.

FIORELLO   Look here now. Why do you keep following me
around? You think I need somebody to hold my hand?

MORRIS   It's a black night for all of us, Major.
> (FIORELLO, *embarrassed and touched, walks away, then
> comes back and speaks quietly*)

FIORELLO   You go home now. It's good to have friends. I appreciate it. But I want to be alone now. (*They start out, each saying
"Good night." Suddenly his manner changes. He becomes dy-
namic*) We'll work.

MORRIS (*Turns*)   What is it, Major?

FIORELLO   There's work to do. Everyone gets hit in the head
with a baseball bat once in a while. Sometimes twice in succes-
sion. I don't want to feel sorry for myself and I don't want you
to feel sorry for me. (*Points*) They're out there and we'll fight

them. If we can't fight them in City Hall, we'll fight them in the courts. I'll see you in the office tomorrow morning at nine o'clock.

MORRIS   Yes, Major. Good night.
   (*They exit.* FIORELLO *is alone on the stage*)

FIORELLO (*Sings "The Name's LaGuardia"*)
   The name's LaGuardia
   L-A-G-U-A-R-D-I-A!
   (*He strides off*)

Blackout

Place: The main room of the Ben Marino Association on West Third Street. Over the same large round poker table, covered with green baize, still hangs the same single electric bulb shielded by one of those porcelain shades that look like ice-cream cones; white on the inside, green on the outside. In the background, through a haze of cigar smoke, we can still see all the other recognizable symbols of a battered, musty political meeting house.

At rise: BEN'S POLITICAL HACKS *are still seated around the table. They are still playing five-card stud.*

FIRST HACK These poor Tammany crooks must have bad dreams about Judge Seabury every night.
(*Laughter.* BEN *deals*)

SECOND HACK (*Reading from a newspaper*) Listen. Then after he gets this joker on the stand and he's sworn in, Judge Seabury says, "From 1929 when Mayor Walker appointed you till today in 1933 your official salary totaled forty thousand dollars."

BEN "Will you please tell the investigating committee how you were able to maintain a Wall Street brokerage account?"

THIRD HACK No, that was the Commissioner of Hospitals yesterday.

SECOND HACK With this boy it's a seventy-five-thousand-dollar mansion in Teaneck, New Jersey.

THIRD HACK   And you know where he got it?

BEN (*Grinning*)   Out of a little tin box his wife keeps on the kitchen shelf.
> (*He gets up and takes the newspaper*)

SECOND HACK   That's right.

BEN (*Slapping newspaper*)   Give 'em hell, Judge. Give 'em hell.

SECOND HACK   Your witness!
> (*They sing "Little Tin Box"*)

FOURTH HACK

> Mr. "X," may we ask you a question?
> It's amazing is it not?
> That the city pays you slightly less
> Than fifty bucks a week
> Yet you've purchased a private yacht!

BEN

> I am positive Your Honor must be joking
> Any working man can do what I have done
> For a month or two I simply gave up smoking
> And I put my extra pennies one by one

> Into a little tin box
> A little tin box
> That a little tin key unlocks
> There is nothing unorthodox
> About a little tin box

MEN

> About a little tin box
> About a little tin box

In a little tin box
A little tin box
That a little tin key unlocks

BEN

There is honor and purity

ALL

Lots of security
In a little tin box

FIFTH HACK (*Speaking*)   Next witness.

FIRST HACK

Mr. "Y," we've been told you don't feel well
And we know you've lost your voice
But we wonder how you managed on the salary you make
To acquire a new Rolls Royce

BEN

You're implying I'm a crook and I say no sir!
There is nothing in my past I care to hide
I've been taking empty bottles to the grocer
And each nickel that I got was put aside

MEN

That he got was put aside

BEN

Into a little tin box
A little tin box
That a little tin key unlocks
There is nothing unorthodox
About a little tin box

MEN

    About a little tin box
    About a little tin box
    In a little tin box
    A little tin box
    There's a cushion for life's rude shocks

BEN

    There is faith, hope and charity

ALL

    Hard-won prosperity
    In a little tin box.

FIFTH HACK (*Speaking*)   Next witness! Take the stand!

SIXTH HACK

    Mr. "Z," you're a junior official
    And your income's rather low
    Yet you've kept a dozen women
    In the very best hotels
    Would you kindly explain, how so?

BEN

    I can see Your Honor doesn't pull his punches
    And it looks a trifle fishy, I'll admit
    But for one whole week I went without my lunches
    And it mounted up, Your Honor, bit by bit

MEN

    Up Your Honor, bit by bit.
    It's just a little tin box
    A little tin box
    That a little tin key unlocks

There is nothing unorthodox
About a little tin box
About a little tin box
About a little tin box
In a little tin box
A little tin box
All a-glitter with blue chip stocks

BEN

There is something delectable

ALL

Almost respectable
In a little tin box
In a little tin box!

BEN (*Speaking*) Tammany won't roll over and play dead.

THIRD HACK But if we get the right man—

FIRST HACK Who is it, Ben? Who we gonna run?

BEN We're gonna run just exactly whoever Judge Seabury picks to run.

SECOND HACK LaGuardia?

BEN I hope not. Maybe Frank Streeter.

FOURTH HACK He's a Democrat.

BEN It's a Fusion ticket.

SECOND HACK What'll we get out of it?

BEN   That's what I'm gonna be told this afternoon.
 (MARIE *enters*)

MARIE   Hello.

BEN   Well, Miss Fischer.

MARIE   Hello, Ben. Boys.

SECOND HACK (*Shaking hands*)   Long time no see.

MARIE   Ed.

BEN   Social or business?

MARIE   What?

BEN   Come over here with a message of any kind?

MARIE   Oh, my, no. I came over to see you personally.

BEN   Have a seat.

FIRST HACK   See you later, eh, Ben?
 (*The men start to straggle out*)

BEN   I'll be here.

SEVENTH HACK   Good to see you, Marie.
 (*The men go.* BEN *pulls up a chair near* MARIE *and sits*)

BEN   So?

MARIE   Ben, Mr. LaGuardia needs you.

BEN   His bootblack quit?

MARIE   I think he might be running for office again. He needs your advice. He needs your criticism.

BEN   My criticism? Oh, sure. He thrives on that!

MARIE   He does thrive on it. You know he has a deep affection for you.

BEN   Has he mentioned my name once in three years? (*No answer*) I thought so.

MARIE   We all know what he is.

BEN   A megalomaniac, that's what he is—and I've had it.

MARIE   Oh, Ben, you're too big for that—honestly—don't you want to beat Tammany?

BEN   I do—with a candidate who appreciates me. Good God, Marie. I should think you'd have had it, too. You going to wait around for him all your life?

MARIE   No, I'm not. (MORRIS *enters*) After this campaign, I'm quitting, but that doesn't mean I won't always be loyal to him.

MORRIS   Hello.

BEN   What is this? A class reunion? Hi, Morris.
      (*They shake hands.* SEVENTH HACK *pokes his head in the* door)

SEVENTH HACK   Ben, Frank Streeter—on the phone.
      (*He pulls his head out*)

BEN   Make yourselves at home.
      (*He hurries out*)

131

MARIE   Did you find out?

MORRIS   I did.

MARIE   Well?

MORRIS   The answer is yes.

MARIE   Oh, Morris, isn't that exciting. Now we've got to do something. We've got to.

MORRIS   What did you mean telling him you're quitting?

MARIE   Morris, I talk too much. Now when Ben gets back—

MORRIS   You're quitting what? Quitting the office?

MARIE   This isn't the place to talk about my private troubles.

MORRIS   We've got to wait for Ben, so we've got to talk about something. Sit down. Have a cigar. Quitting what?

MARIE   Nothing, nothing, Morris, please!

MORRIS   You're among friends.

MARIE   Oh, I know that. You heard the Major yelling at me this morning, I suppose—

MORRIS   Sure.

MARIE   I'd made a date the night before.

MORRIS   Date?

MARIE   He didn't like it! I had my hat and coat on, ready to leave the office, and he wanted me to stay while he redictated a brief. (*Music plays softly*) Remember the last time we were here? Morris, I want to get married.

MORRIS   Sure.

MARIE   I've been taking a long hard look at life.

MORRIS   You're really serious?

MARIE   Yes, pal, I'm out to catch a husband—and I think making dates is the way to do it.

MORRIS   That's how Shirley caught me.

MARIE   So far, they've all bored me to tears—but I'll keep trying.

MORRIS   You'll never be able to quit.

MARIE   Won't I?

MORRIS   No.
   (MARIE *sings "The Very Next Man"*)

MARIE
   I shall marry the very next man who asks me,
   You'll see.
   Next time I feel
   That a man's about to kneel
   He won't have to plead or implore
   I'll say "yes" before his knee hits the floor.

   No more waiting around
   No more browsing through *True Romance*

FIORELLO!

I've seen the light so while there's a chance
I'm gonna marry the very next man
Who asks me.

Start rehearsing the choir
Tie some shoes on my Chevrolet
Pelt me with rice and catch my bouquet
I'm gonna marry the very next man

If he adores me
What does it matter if he bores me?
If I allow the man to carry me off
No more will people try to marry me off

No more living alone
No more cheating at solitaire
Holding my breath for one special man
Why I could smother for all he'd care
I'm through being wary
I'll marry the very next man

No more daydreams for me
Find the finest of bridal suites
Chill the champagne and warm up the sheets
I'm gonna marry the very next man

And if he likes me
Who cares how frequently he strikes me
I'll fetch his slippers with my arm in a sling
Just for the privilege of wearing his ring

New York papers, take note!
Here's a statement that you can quote:

Waiting for ships that never come in
A girl is likely to miss the boat
I'm through being wary
I'll marry the very next man.
   (BEN MARINO *enters*)

BEN   Well, boys and girls, I just had a very cooperative talk with a certain candidate for Mayor. Honest but grateful.

MARIE   Ben, I've got to tell you something. If Mr. LaGuardia will take it, he's to get the nomination—that's definite.

BEN   How would you know?
   (MARIE *nods toward* MORRIS)

MORRIS   I got a cousin who works in the stenographic pool at Seabury's office. I just came from there. Seabury's going to proposition the Major tomorrow morning.

BEN   You don't say.

MORRIS   Of course, I'm not sure he'll accept.

BEN   He always accepts.

MARIE   He's in a very strange mood, Ben. But if you came to him, if you were in his office tomorrow at ten, I think he would.

BEN   Tell him to call me. Tell him to get in touch.

MARIE   Ben, he can't. You know him as well as we do. He can't. Now don't be such a stubborn fool.

BEN   Good God, you sound like Fiorello. It's catching.

MARIE   Wouldn't it be fun to start another campaign? All together? I'm going to call some of the leaders from the other districts. I know they'll come. It's too good to miss. You've got to be there.
(*The poker players straggle in*)

FOURTH HACK   We too early?

BEN   Not at all. Shuffle the cards. I'll be right with you.

THIRD HACK   Who's dealing?

FOURTH HACK   Ben is.

MARIE   We'll see you, eh, Ben?

BEN   Now wait a minute, I didn't say so.

MARIE   Good-bye.

MORRIS   Good-bye, Ben.

BEN   Good-bye.
(MARIE *and* MORRIS *go*)

SECOND HACK   (*With newspaper*)   Guess who Seabury has got on the rack now?

BEN   I'll tell you who. Me.
(*They sing "Politics and Poker"*)

ALL
Politics and poker
Politics and poker
Everyone is broke

136

And getting broker
Everybody knows
The trouble that we're in
So here we sit playing at poker and politics
Waiting to nominate a candidate
Who's good enough and smart enough
And strong enough to win.

Blackout

Place: FIORELLO'S *office.*

At rise: When the lights come on, we are interested in the outer office, where NEIL *is sitting at his desk, talking on the phone. In the inner office, dimly seen, are* FIORELLO, *at his desk, and* MRS. POMERANTZ, *sitting in front of it.*

NEIL (*Into phone*) Me on a committee? I don't understand. No, Mr. LaGuardia hasn't said anything to me about it. Well, yes, sure, I can be reached at this number, but— Sure. Yes. Okay. (*He hangs up and turns to* MORRIS) Morris, is the Major going back into politics?

MORRIS Why do you ask?

NEIL Some guy from Judge Seabury's office just called me about being on a fund-raising committee for this Fusion ticket I been reading about.

FLORENCE (*Looking up from the switchboard*) Neil, excuse me, but I got somebody asking for a Mr. Ben Marino?

NEIL Ben Marino hasn't been in this office for three years.
(*The lights come up in the inner office and our attention is directed to* FIORELLO *and* MRS. POMERANTZ)

FIORELLO Mrs. Pomerantz, if I succeed in getting Noonan into court, you'll get your money. I guarantee that. The question is purely one of time.

MRS. POMERANTZ By me also. Forty years I'm saving my Lennie should be a doctor.

FIORELLO I'll do my best, Mrs. Pomerantz. But the law doesn't always move as fast as we'd like.

MRS. POMERANTZ The best, naturally, this I know you'll do, like always. But the law for once you'll have to give it a little bit a shake.
   (*The phone rings.* FIORELLO *picks it up*)

FIORELLO Yes?

NEIL (*On the phone in the outer office*) Major—the Noonan case has been taken off the docket.

FIORELLO (*Into phone*) I'll talk to you in one minute. (*He hangs up*) All right, Mrs. Pomerantz, just try to be patient.
   (*He rises*)

MRS. POMERANTZ (*Rising*) Me, I'm patient—but the clock—?

FIORELLO I'll call you.
   (*He shows her to the outer office*)

MRS. POMERANTZ (*To* FIORELLO, *as* NEIL *comes in*) So please, do me a favor, don't get sick till Lennie graduates. From then on, the rest of your life, you should live to be a hundred and twenty, a doctor's bill you'll never have to pay.
   (*She exits. The moment* MRS. POMERANTZ *disappears,* FIORELLO's *manner changes. He turns angrily*)

FIORELLO (*Pointing at* NEIL) Now say that again! I don't think I heard you right. The Noonan case has been taken off the docket?

NEIL (*Nervous*)   Yes, sir.

FIORELLO (*Thunders*)   Why?

NEIL   The clerk of the court—said he didn't know why—except that it was done by order of Judge Carter.

FIORELLO (*Sharp*)   Which Judge Carter?

NEIL   Joseph F., sir.

FIORELLO (*Incredulous*)   General Sessions?

NEIL   Yes, sir.

FIORELLO (*Roars*)   What the hell is a General Sessions judge doing with the New York Supreme Court docket?

MORRIS (*Enters with an armful of folders, speaks quietly*)   Why don't you ask Jimmy Hines?

FIORELLO (*Angry*)   He's not on my staff! You two are!

MORRIS (*Laying down the folders one by one on* FIORELLO's *desk*) The same thing that happened on Bienstock versus Cowan. Delfino versus Eberhardt. Fisher versus Geoghan. And the four billion others we've worked on these last three years. It's hopeless.

FIORELLO   Nothing is hopeless. Haven't you worked here long enough to learn that?

MORRIS   I've worked here long enough to learn the difference between law and politics.

FIORELLO (*Scornfully sarcastic*) A Solomon—a Solomon come
to judgment!

MORRIS You don't think I'm right?

FIORELLO Of course you're right!
(MARIE *enters the outer office*)

MARIE Florence, were there any men asking for me?

FLORENCE No, but there were some messages.
(*She hands message slips to* MARIE)

FIORELLO If any crook has a friend at the Wigwam he doesn't
have to go to court. Don't you think I see the termites eating
up my city? Don't you think I know something should be
done? God damn it, you were there. You've been with us.
Didn't I try? (MARIE *is attracted to his door by his loud voice.*
She knocks) Well! (MARIE *enters*) All right, get out, you two
—I'll talk to you later. (MORRIS *and* NEIL *exit. To* MARIE) I'm
sorry. I don't know what's come over me these days.

MARIE (*Quiet*) I do. (*He turns to look at her*) If a person loves
something—or somebody—as much as you love this city, Mr.
LaGuardia, it's not easy to stand by and watch, without saying
a word, or lifting a finger—

FIORELLO (*Shakes his head wearily*) I can't, Marie. I can't.
They turned their backs on me. They didn't want me.

MARIE That's not true, Mr. LaGuardia. They didn't turn their
backs on you. They just weren't looking. They didn't have to
look. They were making too much money. They were having
too much fun. But things are different now. The fun is over.
People are starving. They'll listen now, Mr. LaGuardia.

FIORELLO   I'm awfully tired, Marie.

MARIE (*Taking her courage in her hands*)   No, you're not. You're scared. (*His head comes up sharply*) You're afraid they'll turn their backs on you again. That's what's wrong. You're scared you'll lose a second time.
    (*He glares at her. She is frightened but she stands her ground and stares back at him. The lights come up in the outer office*)

FIRST HACK (*Enters and addresses* FLORENCE)   Is Mr. Ben Marino here?

FLORENCE   No, sir, he hasn't been here in three years.

FIRST HACK   I know that. What about Miss Fischer?

FLORENCE   What's the name please?

FIRST HACK   I have an appointment with Mr. Ben Marino. (MARIE *enters*) Oh—here she is.

MARIE (*Shaking hands with* FIRST HACK)   Hello, Ed. The others will be here shortly.
    (BEN *enters behind them*)

BEN   Well, the old place hasn't changed such a hell of a lot.

MARIE   Thank you for coming.

BEN   I'll probably get thrown out, but I always enjoy short visits.
    (*Two other men enter behind them*)

FIRST MAN   Oh, here he is.

BEN   Hello, Ed. Hello, Louis.

SECOND MAN   Hi ya, Ben. We got a quorum?

NEIL   Ben—Ben Marino! Well!

BEN   Morris! Neil!

MORRIS   How are you, Ben?
   (FIORELLO *appears in the doorway of his private office*)

FIORELLO   Who? (*Stops in astonishment*) Well, this is a great honor. What the hell are you doing in this office?

BEN   I came to help, Fiorello.

FIORELLO   Help? Has somebody around here been asking for help? Help what?

BEN   Help you in your next campaign.

FIORELLO   I have no campaign.

BEN   Hasn't Judge Seabury talked to you?

FIORELLO   I give him a little advice once in a while. Of course, he's talked to me.

BEN   About running for Mayor?

FIORELLO   No, not exactly.

BEN   On a Fusion ticket. You know what I'm talking about.

MORRIS (*Close behind* FIORELLO)   Judge Carter, Special Sessions.

FIORELLO (*Wheels on him*) What did you say?

MORRIS I think you said it, Major. Nothing is hopeless.
(*Politicians enter from outside*)

POLITICIAN Well, here we are.

FIORELLO More politicians, huh?

FLORENCE Excuse me, Mr. LaGuardia. Judge Seabury is on the phone.
(*The room is very quiet.* FIORELLO *hesitates, then turns toward the door of his inner office. He stops and comes back*)

FIORELLO And if I should decide to run again, I want all you politicians to know that my chief qualification for Mayor of this great city is my monumental ingratitude.
(*He goes into the office and picks up the phone and is seen in conversation during the following*)

BEN The old fire-eater hasn't changed such a hell of a lot.

MARIE Do you want him to?

BEN What good'll it do me?

MORRIS Hooray!
(*He throws the files on the floor*)

BEN What's the matter with you?

MORRIS I'm happy! We're going to run again!
(*He begins an impromptu dance.* FIORELLO *hangs up the phone, comes into the outer office.* MORRIS *stops dancing.*

All stare at FIORELLO. *He points at* MARIE. *She follows him into his inner office*)

BEN (*Laughing*) That guy kills me. He just plain kills me. (*More politicians appear from outside*) Come in, boys.
(*Lights come up in the inner office, where* MARIE *stands penitently waiting to hear what* FIORELLO *has to say*)

FIORELLO Did you ask Ben Marino to come here?

MARIE Yes, I thought—

FIORELLO Thought what? That I couldn't do my own thinking?

MARIE Thought if you were going to run for Mayor, you'd need friends. True friends, like Ben.

FIORELLO It's nice to know you're taking over running my life. You're getting very independent lately.

MARIE I'm sorry.
(*There is a pause. She starts back for the outer office. He calls her*)

FIORELLO Wait a minute—come here. You're fired!

MARIE Fired?

FIORELLO As of now.

MARIE Just because I—?

FIORELLO No. The reason is different. I can't court a girl who's working for me.

145

MARIE   Mr. LaGuardia!

FIORELLO   Will you marry me? (*She moves away from him and sits down. Music starts softly*) I know it's kind of sudden.

MARIE   Sudden! Yes, it is.

FIORELLO   But, honestly, Marie, I think you can learn to love me.

MARIE   Yes, I think I can. I've been practicing for fifteen years.

FIORELLO (*Speaking*)
Good. It's a deal. I've got plans, Marie. I'm not very good at expressing my feelings, but I'm good at making plans. We have so many things to share, so much in common. It's going to be all right, Marie—dear Marie.

MARIE (*Singing*)
Start rehearsing the choir
Tie some shoes on my Chevrolet
Pelt me with rice and catch my bouquet, for I start changing my name today
I'm through being wary
I'll marry the very next man.

(*Politicians sing in the outer office*)

MEN (*Soft*)
We want LaGuardia
L-A-G-U-A-R-D-I-A
(*Loud*)
We want LaGuardia
L-A-G-U-A-R-D-I-A!
(MARIE *takes* FIORELLO's *hand and leads him into the outer office. He faces the politicians and raises his arms to indicate that he will accept the nomination to run again*

for Mayor of New York. MARIE *beams. The politicians
sing lustily)*
Let every racketeer and reprobate
Start to say a silent prayer
We've got the man who's going to turn the town
Both inside out and upside down
LaGuardia! His Honor the Mayor!
Yes, you can change it all
The people want you to
So cast your spell come next Election Day
The name's LaGuardia
L-A-G-U-A-R-D-I-A!

Curtain